I thoroughly enjoyed reading this book. I believe it will be a great source of encouragement and hope for young moms. Full of practical advice, applications, and real-life stories, it's a great reminder to be a future-thinker and trust that with God's help, what seems impossible can become reality.

— Erin O'Donnell

A life interrupted can become a life ignited. Trish Goyer provides the path to help and hope for young moms in this exceptional book. When Carol Kuykendall and I wrote *What Every Mom Needs* over a decade ago, our prayer was that moms would become better moms by learning to recognize and meet their needs. Now this message comes home to even the youngest of moms in a tone and language that connects. From Teen MOPS to classic MOPS, this book works.

— Elisa Morgan, President and CEO, MOPS International,

ds

D1119441

life interrupted

*May you find
HOPE!
Tricia Goyer*

Resources from MOPS

Books
  Beyond Macaroni and Cheese
  The Birthday Book
  Children Change a Marriage
  A Cure for the Growly Bugs and Other Tips for Moms
  Loving and Letting Go
  Make Room for Daddy
  Meditations for Mothers
  Mom to Mom
  Mom's Health Matters
  A Mother's Footprints of Faith
  Real Moms
  What Every Child Needs
  What Every Mom Needs

Books with Drs. Henry Cloud and John Townsend
  Raising Great Kids
  Raising Great Kids for Parents of Preschoolers Workbook
  Raising Great Kids for Parents of School-Age Children Workbook
  Raising Great Kids for Parents of Teenagers Workbook

Gift Books
  God's Words of Life from the Mom's Devotional Bible

Kids Books
  Boxes, Boxes Everywhere
  Mad Maddie Maxwell
  Mommy, May I Hug the Fishes?
  My Cowboy Boots
  Mud Pie Annie
  See the Country, See the City
  Sister for Sale
  Snug as a Bug?
  Zachary's Zoo

Bible
  Mom's Devotional Bible

Audio Pages®
  Raising Great Kids

Curriculum
  Raising Great Kids for Parents of Preschoolers ZondervanGroupware™
    (with Drs. Henry Cloud and John Townsend)

MOTHERS OF
M✦PS®
PRESCHOOLERS
...because mothering matters

life interrupted

the scoop
on being
a young mom

tricia goyer

ZONDERVAN™

GRAND RAPIDS, MICHIGAN 49530 USA

ZONDERVAN™

Life Interrupted
Copyright © 2004 by Tricia Goyer

Requests for information should be addressed to:
Zondervan, *Grand Rapids, Michigan 49530*

Library of Congress Cataloging-in-Publication Data

Goyer, Tricia.
    Life interrupted : the scoop on being a young mom / Tricia Goyer.
       p. cm.
    Includes bibliographical references.
    ISBN 0-310-25316-0
    1. Teenage mothers—Religious life. 2. Unmarried mothers—Religious life.
  I. Title.
    BV4529.18.G69 2004
    248.8'33—dc22
                                        2004004686

Interior design by Beth Shagene

Printed in the United States of America

---

04 05 06 07 08 09 10 /❖DC/ 10 9 8 7 6 5 4 3 2 1

To every young mom who hopes for a good future.
You can do it. You matter!

contents

Before I Was a Mom

Before I was a mom,
I hung out on Main Street.
Took pride in my appearance.
Talked for hours on the phone.
And sunbathed for fun.

Before I was a mom,
I stayed up all night.
Slept 'til noon on Saturdays.
Painted my nails.

Before I was a mom,
I kept up with my homework.
Knew all the latest movies.
Watched TV that didn't include
    puppets.

Before I was a mom,
I didn't realize the importance
    of vitamins.
Didn't consider the danger of
    electrical outlets.
Spoke in complete sentences.

Before I was a mom,
I changed my clothes when they
    were stained.
Thought poop was disgusting.
Gagged at drool.
Never imagined sniffing a diaper.

Before I was a mom,
I had big plans for my future.
Looked into college.
Never considered the cost of day
    care.
Had no idea what "effaced" or
    "epidural" meant.

Before I was a mom,
I slept through everything.
Didn't realize how exciting
    crawling could be.
Never thought to videotape
    someone walking.
Didn't know how beautiful
    "mama" sounded.

Before I was a mom,
I never watched a baby sleep.
Never appreciated a soft giggle.
Never knew how much love I had
    inside.
Never thought one small being
    could change me so completely.

Before I was a mom,
I never realized a feeling so great,
So wonderful,
So intimate,
As loving my own child.
                    —Tricia Goyer

me . . . a mom?

Like most little girls, I imagined marrying a great guy and becoming a mommy. In bed at night I'd let my mind wander, picturing my future family. I loved watching reruns of *The Brady Bunch* and decided I wanted six kids too. My guy would be the best of TV hubbies wrapped into one: handsome, funny, kind, and always understanding. (Rich wouldn't hurt either!)

I also imagined the day I'd tell my husband I was expecting. He would come home from work to our white cottage with green shutters, and I'd have a candlelight dinner waiting. Baby back ribs, baby carrots, and baby peas, of course. I'd be glowing—not from the candlelight, but from the "joy of expectancy." My husband would look at me with one eyebrow cocked. I would nod enthusiastically and we'd embrace. After dinner we'd head to the mall to pick out our first baby outfit. *Perfect.*

Reality check! What really happened was quite different.

I was seventeen. I was riding home from the doctor's office with my mom, and I felt like puking. I bet my mother did too! I was her little girl, but now I was going to be a mom. We both were clueless about where to go from there.

As we drove, I saw a familiar car heading the other direction.

"There he is," I blurted.

My mom flipped a U-turn. We followed the dented Nova into the McDonald's parking lot. Another girl shared Rob's (not his real name) front seat.

I jumped out and marched to his car. "We need to talk."

13

The chick glanced the other way, and he followed me back behind the dumpster.

I looked into his eyes. His gaze was ice cold. I glanced at the lips I had kissed a thousand times. They were pressed into a thin line. This was the person I'd dated for three years, but things had begun to stink. Neither of us had been happy together. We had a love-hate relationship. We hated the way we treated each other, so we broke up. But we loved getting back together. This time I knew "back together" wouldn't happen.

"What do you want? We decided it was over, remember." He folded his arms across his chest.

"I'm pregnant," I told him flat out.

His expression didn't change. "I don't believe you."

My hands protectively covered my stomach. I raised my voice. "Fine, don't believe me. I don't need you anyway. This baby doesn't need you."

That was one of the last times I talked to him.

One day I was your typical high school senior. An honor student, a cheerleader, and a yearbook editor. I worked part-time at McDonald's to pay for gas and clothes.

The next day, I was a mother-to-be. I knew lots of people who had babies, even a few at my school. But what would it mean for *me?*

One thing I knew sure—I wanted to have this baby. See, this wasn't the first time I'd been pregnant. It had happened once before, a few years prior. My boyfriend and I were new in our relationship, very much in "love," and *young*. I got pregnant when I was fifteen, and we both thought the best solution was an abortion.

Big mistake.

After the abortion, something inside me shut down. I couldn't deal with my emotions, so I flipped them off like a light switch. That's when our relationship took a rocky road. I hated myself for deciding to put my life first over my child's. And every time I was with my boyfriend, he was a reminder of what I'd done.

Yet, here I was again. Same song, different verse.

The second time around, I dealt with my pregnancy by hiding from the world. I couldn't cope with going to school—especially since my "condition" stuck out in front of me wherever I went. So I dropped out of regular high school and attended a community school for troubled teens. (I was a perfect candidate.) I even quit my part-time job at McDonald's because the smell of the food cooking made me sick.

Within a couple of months, my personal life nauseated me. I went nowhere, did nothing. My so-called friends continued on with their senior year. And my boyfriend, as I said, was out of the picture.

I also have to admit I was my own worst enemy. I was lonely and scared. Grumpy and standoffish. I felt like a kid but now I had a huge responsibility. *Me, a mother?*

. . . .

Your New Reality

Does my situation sound familiar? If you're like most young moms, you struggle with a huge lifestyle makeover and major anxieties, not to mention work and school burdens. Relationships with parents, friends, and boyfriends are shaky (8.0 on the Richter scale). This isn't how you imagined your youth!

Then there's your baby, the joy of your life. There's nothing you wouldn't do for your child. Still, your mind wanders to how things *would be* if you hadn't gotten pregnant—normal high school days, parties, friends, the prom. Mothering wasn't supposed to happen this soon.

One of my friends faced the same thing. Her boyfriend was out of the picture right away too. Scared, she didn't tell her mom for three months.

"I knew my mom would be disappointed," Jamie told me as we swapped teen pregnancy stories. "And she was. But my dad was worse. He didn't talk to me for almost my whole pregnancy. Not a phone call, nothing."

But like me, Jamie found the reality of motherhood the hardest thing to deal with. "The thing that keeps me up at night is the idea that I'm a mother," Jamie confessed. "Me, a mom! I just can't believe it."

Maybe you're like Jamie and you envisioned a husband who'd adore you and a neighborhood of friends you'd meet at the park for play dates, *someday in the future*. Then those two pink lines on a pregnancy test changed everything.

Your hopes. Your dreams. Your reality.

Tricia's Blab — Listen Up

While pregnant, you may be surprised how demanding your baby is already. The little baby's awake when you want to sleep. And what's up with camping out on your bladder?

As one pregnant mom put it, "From early on my baby wouldn't stop kicking my ribs — as if he were saying. 'I'm here, and I'm not going away!'"

Think about your pregnancy. What's the one thing that surprised you the most? For me it was the amazing realization that another person was growing inside me. *Wow, imagine that!*

Now, what was the one thing that scared you the most?

. . . Yeah, that scared me too!

What It's Like to Be a Young Mom

If you're like me, you couldn't wait for your due date. Finally, a chance to see this new little person. Like unwrapping a special gift at Christmas, you couldn't wait to see who was inside.

I imagine that the gift was even more than you expected. Wide eyes that trust you completely. A tiny fist around your finger. A pint-size smile. And soft coos. You've fallen in love forever.

But after only a few months (or minutes!) of being a mom, you realize there's no turning back. Your child is a living, breathing person with needs . . . *many* needs. You don't want to think about the next eighteen years . . . perhaps you just want to make it to *your* eighteenth birthday!

A meal tray at McDonald's is a good illustration of what it's like to be a young mom. It doesn't matter how much you order, the goal of the fast-food worker is to make everything fit on *one* tray. Hamburgers, fries, drinks, straws, napkins, ketchup—and who could forget apple pie?

If you're successful, you make it to the table with hardly a fry hitting the floor. But with the slightest bump . . . there goes your super-sized Diet Coke.

Perhaps before pregnancy your "tray" was manageable. You had space for your studies, friends, sports, and maybe even a trip to the beach or ski slopes. Then came baby. You're still a student, daughter, friend, and perhaps girlfriend. And as much as you don't like labels, phrases like *working mother, wife,* or *single parent* now represent you. The space on the tray hasn't increased, but more responsibilities have been stuffed onto it. And if you've ever compared the size of a Happy Meal with a cheeseburger, you know kids require the most space of all.

Your Unique Needs

Needs are like warning signals. They insist on getting our attention. Think of a nuclear power plant. The warning lights and sirens let operators know when something's malfunctioning. If the warnings aren't heeded, there will soon be a meltdown of dangerous proportions.

Your questions, your fears, your lack of knowing what to do—these are like warning signals in your life. They have to be addressed from the inside out. Or, you guessed it, meltdown.

That's why this book is for you! By realizing your needs and working to meet them, you will become a better person and a better mom. I'll address your nine unique needs and show that you're not alone. Yes, there will always be challenges, but this isn't the *end* of life as you know it. Instead, think of this as the *beginning* of a new adventure . . . motherhood.

Back to My Motherhood Story . . .

I gave birth to my son three weeks after graduation. If you think those graduation gowns are unfashionable, imagine how they'd look on someone eight months pregnant!

So you can see that I'm writing this book as one who's been there. Someone who has felt the stares of a condemning world. Someone who dropped out of high school and graduated through alternative education. Someone who had to face the heartbreak of seeing *him* with *her*—the hot, not-pregnant, new girlfriend.

I'm also writing as one who has found success and joy in the years beyond teen parenting. I married a wonderful man, had two more kids, embarked on a successful writing career. I even launched a young moms' support group in my town.

But the road between "there" and "here" wasn't easy. I wish my story played out like a children's book: The pregnant princess meets

Prince Charming. Then she marries him and goes to live in his castle. They live happily ever after. The end.

Instead, my story is like a novel full of troubles and triumphs—both of which I'll share with you in this book.

Helping young moms is now part of my story. Every week I meet with young moms at a group called Teen MOPS (Mothers of Preschoolers), to provide support and encouragement. And you know what? Young moms are amazing. They make many sacrifices and face their challenges head-on. Like the young moms in my group, you're trying to make the best of a hard situation. That's why you're reading this book. You go girl!

My goal for this book is to encourage you by sharing my story and the stories of other young moms. I also want to provide advice I would have appreciated when I was a new mother at seventeen.

Finally, my ultimate purpose for this book is to help you make *your story* the best it can be. Yes, you will face challenges on your mothering journey, but I hope the encouragement you'll find within these pages will help you ensure there will be much success too.

Let's get started!

1

do I matter?
importance

The deepest principle in the human nature is the craving to be appreciated.

— William James, author

Erica handed the food stamps to the grocery store clerk. She tried to appear natural, as if it didn't bother her that the government, not she, supported her child. Two-month-old Kayla lay fastened in the shopping-cart baby seat. The clerk had smiled at the baby but didn't ask Erica any of the friendly questions new mothers typically get. Instead, Erica spotted something else in the woman's gaze. Disapproval, with a hint of accusation.

Erica tucked her change into her jacket pocket and loaded her few bags of groceries into the cart. Before reaching the exit Erica noticed an elderly woman approaching. The woman's eyes fastened intently on Kayla. *At least someone's interested in giving my baby some well-deserved attention,* Erica thought.

Kayla's pacifier wiggled up and down with each suck. Erica started to smile as the woman's frail hand reached toward Kayla's face. But instead of stroking the baby's cheek, the woman plucked the pacifier from her mouth.

"That thing's nasty." She dropped it into Erica's trembling hand. "Don't you know not to use those things?" The woman stalked

21

away before Erica could respond. Heat crept up Erica's neck to her face. Ignoring the customers who had witnessed the scene, she hurried to her small, blue hatchback.

Erica struggled to hold back the tears. Did they think she was a bad mother? That she was a failure because of her age?

Erica fastened Kayla in her car seat with a peck on her forehead. She then plopped the groceries into the trunk and slid into the driver's seat.

It was always the same. The looks. The comments. The lack of respect. Even a few weeks ago at the doctor's office, her valid concerns for her daughter had been ignored.

"It's just colic," the doctor had claimed, rushing off to visit the next low-income patient. It was only Erica's persistence, days later, which brought more tests and a better diagnosis. Having a baby at her age was difficult enough, but the reactions of those around her made being a mother all that much harder.

What if they're right? she wondered. *What if I can't do this? What if they know something I don't?*

Erica thought back to just one year ago. She'd worked hard at school and her report card reflected those efforts. She'd trained her body to perform on the soccer field. The stellar plays and winning season were her rewards.

What about this motherhood thing? She tried to do it right. Erica gave her baby plenty of time, attention, and love. She even practiced the baby massage techniques she'd learned in her Teen MOPS group. But was her hard work paying off? How could she know when there was no report card or scoreboard to judge her efforts?

Erica's hands gripped the steering wheel as she thought back to the question she'd heard many times. "Just how old are you?" She always told the truth, and she always received the same look of disapproval. Perhaps these people at the grocery store, at the doctor's office, knew something she didn't.

Erica glanced back at Kayla, now asleep in her car seat. Could she do it? This mom thing? Or was she just a kid playing dress up, fooling no one except herself?

Life as I See It

I do feel inadequate. I cry sometimes and have even had a few anxiety attacks, but therapy is a luxury for us working poor.

— Travis, Michigan

Some people have given me dirty looks when they see me with my baby. Others look at me and sigh. But some people are very nice when they see what a good mom I am.

— Diana, Washington

. . . .

Life Interrupted

> I'm finding it very overrated, all of this growing up, taking responsibility, becoming an adult.
>
> — Brandon, *90210*

These were supposed to be years of parties, football games, and fun. Dances with handsome dates and sleepovers with friends. You've gone from chatting with friends in the hall to changing dirty diapers. Not long ago, the only runny nose you wiped was your own. Colic wasn't an issue. Your clothes were spit-up free. Now you wonder where your importance is.

When your baby came into the picture you not only lost your old life, but you gained a new one — literally. Many of us know, without a doubt, that having our babies was the right choice. We want to be good moms. We want to give our babies the love that we, perhaps, never had. But if we're honest, we can't help but think how our lives have changed. Sometimes we wonder if it's worth it.

Life as I See It

When I found out I was pregnant, I was incredibly scared and didn't know how to tell my parents. They'd always said they'd kill me if I ever ended up pregnant.

— Desiree, Texas

Before my pregnancy, I was in four clubs and had a meeting almost every night. Most of my friends have completely left the picture. I figured they would, but I feel very alone. Having a baby has really helped me to see who my real friends are.

— Amanda, Ontario, Canada

Tell Me I'm Important

Young moms want to be good moms. We try our best, we really do. Yet there are negative reactions we can't seem to escape. We've decided to carry and keep our babies (not an easy decision!). But often the people we encounter make it clear, both in words and with body language, that they disapprove. Sometimes we feel like we have no importance.

But I'm here to tell you that what you do is *important*. Can you think of anyone who loves your child more than you do? I doubt that you can! You're the exact person your child needs to love him, support him, and be his biggest fan.

Did Ya Know?

Importance means having meaning. There are many things that people feel are important for young people: school, good grades, sports, and clubs.

What things were important to you one or two years ago? What things are important now?

Parenting comes with big obstacles. Yet as you'll see in a story often told, sometimes human beings can do the impossible when it comes to their child.

. . . .

Moving Mountains

"There were two warring tribes in the Andes, one that lived in the lowlands and the other high in the mountains. The mountain people invaded the lowlanders one day, and as part of their plundering of the people, they kidnapped a baby from one of the lowlander families and took the infant back with them up into the mountains.

"The lowlanders didn't know how to climb a mountain. They didn't know any of the trails the mountain people used, and they didn't know where to find the mountain people or how to track them on the steep terrain.

"Even so, they sent out their best party of fighting men to climb the mountain and bring the baby home.

"The men tried first one method of climbing and then another. They tried one trail and then another. After several days of effort, however, they had climbed only a couple of hundred feet.

"Feeling hopeless and helpless, the lowlander men decided that the case was lost, and they prepared to return to their village below.

"As they were packing their gear for the descent, they saw the baby's mother walking toward them. They realized that she was coming down the mountain that they hadn't figured out how to climb.

"And then they saw that she had the baby strapped to her back. How could that be?

"One man greeted her and said, 'We couldn't climb this mountain. How did you do this when we, the strongest and most able men in the village, couldn't do it?'

"She shrugged her shoulders and said, 'It wasn't your baby.'"[1]

You're a mom now, and the obstacles you face may seem as big and insurmountable as that mountain. But there's one thing that's even more powerful than your challenges. That's your love. Love is the most important ingredient when it comes to parenting. Love, as you will discover, can help you to achieve the impossible.

Help! My Life Is Slipping Away

> If you bungle raising your children, I don't think whatever else you do well matters very much.
> — Jacqueline Kennedy Onassis[2]

Just because a mom's willing to do *anything* for her child, doesn't mean it's easy. Motherhood can be illustrated by an image of a woman wearing a tower of hats. There is the nurse's hat, the teacher's hat, the maid's hat, the cook's hat, the playmate's hat—the list goes on. As a young mom, your problem may be the many hats you haven't discarded: the student hat, employee hat, girlfriend hat, even the daughter-at-home hat. How can you—one person—balance so much responsibility?

Life as I See It

I get so tired of people asking, "How old are you?" We even had to change pediatricians once because the doctor wouldn't speak to me as an adult. I wanted to yell, "Hey, I am her mother. I'm responsible for her welfare!" I used to cry at night, not because I didn't want this, but because I had no idea how much my life would change.

— Marjie, Montana

When I went into the hospital for my non-stress test the nurse told me that she wanted my baby, and that she would prepare the adoption papers if it was a boy.

— Amanda, Ontario, Canada

Some people haven't treated me any different since I've become a mom. Others talk to me as though I'm stupid, like we're all alcoholic-induced, unplanned mothers, sitting on our butts, contemplating how we can scam the welfare system for more money as we blast our stereo and fill our screaming children with second hand smoke, Kool-Aid, and Doritos.

— Travis, Michigan

Of course, your balancing act will change over time. The hat of high school student may change to that of college student. The playground-mom hat may change to soccer mom. Still, the flow of your responsibilities will never end. From the moment you discover you're pregnant, you're Mom, hats and all, for life.

The reality of being a mom may not hit until you come home from the hospital. The feedings, the schedule, the up-all-nights. Then, as one stage passes, there are more challenges: teething, climbing, the terrible twos, and on.

The worst part is doing it alone. Some young moms have a husband or boyfriend. Perhaps your family helps. Friends may come around now and then. But there are always days when it feels like it's *you and this kid against the world.*

Life as I See It

How do you keep your endurance for mothering alive? How do you stay in mom-mode and stay out of the life your peers are living? How do you stay who you are inside even as parenting takes over your life? Don't get me wrong, I love being a mom. Goodness knows I should have the answers to these questions by now, as my boy is almost two. But lately, I have those feelings where it seems I'm 'left out' again. Like the rest of the world is passing me by while I change a diaper.

— Leanne

Stereotyped by Society

> All the girls drink but I'm the one that gets caught. That's
> the story of my life. I always get the fuzzy end of the
> lollipop.
>
> — Marilyn Monroe, *Some Like It Hot*

So, as we've discussed, it's hard being a good mom and worse
when people judge you because of your age. As if they think you
sleep around with just anyone. They assume you're doomed to fail.

We all, at times, worry what others think. I remember the first
time I stood in a welfare line. I needed help with medical costs,
food, living expenses—you name it. But before going, I made sure I
looked my best. I didn't want to be stereotyped as someone uneducated and unmotivated. I wanted others to respect me, despite the
situation I was in.

Hear Me Out

Ponderings from a Young Mom

Is there a magical age that makes mothering okay? Can I hold my head high
at twenty? Twenty-five? Thirty? What makes a good mom? A nice paycheck? A
house in the suburbs? Will people respect me if I enrolled my child in a private
preschool? Or dressed him in designer clothes?

Or is it enough just to love him? To read stories at bedtime? To kiss baby
toes and tickle baby bellies? It may not be enough for society. But it will be
enough for me. For my child.

When I faced the reality of being a young mother, I could have
given up. I could have accepted that many young moms never graduate from high school and live at poverty level for the rest of their
lives. But inside, I knew I wasn't someone the world could write off.

I simply had found myself in a situation way over my head. I wanted the world to know I was a smart young woman who would love this child completely.

Because of this, I decided to believe in myself and take distasteful looks in stride. I strove to be an anti-stereotype and show the world what a young mom could accomplish.

I realized my importance came from within me. I couldn't please everyone all the time. I couldn't change my situation overnight, but I could take steps to improve. I could work at becoming a great mom. And it worked!

As I believed in myself, and trusted in my importance as a mother, my confidence grew. Like a small snowball kicked over the side of a steep hill, I picked up speed, and grew as a person. Soon I became unstoppable!

Home Life: The Bad, the Good

> Have you noticed that the only people who truly welcome change are wet babies?
>
> — Anonymous

The Bad

It's hard enough that "the world" looks down on you. But what if you face negative attitudes at home? Many young moms who still live with their parents may feel like the cream in the middle of an Oreo cookie. They're sandwiched between their parents and their child. (Only this situation is not sweet.) These young moms are parents, *and* they still live by their parents' rules. These moms get advice from all directions and may feel like they're "mothering by committee."

I hear it all the time from the young moms I know. *Their* mothers want to make all the rules—to tell them how to dress their kids and what to feed their child. Sometimes these young moms feel they've been left out of the decision making.

If this is your case, be sure to try to see your parents' point of view, but also get them to understand yours. It's key that you realize *your importance* as a mother. Once *you* accept your importance, and take responsibility in your new role, hopefully your parents will realize it too.

The Good

For others, becoming a young parent can strengthen family bonds. This was true in my case. Right away my "friends" ditched me. But my family stayed and cared. They stuck by me and believed in me.

My parents and grandparents helped me to realize my importance . . . even on days when I wanted to sleep in and hide from the world! They helped by letting me make my own decisions when it came to parenting. And I soon learned my decisions mattered.

Life as I See It

My mother constantly says, "I love you and the baby, but I wish you had waited until you were done with school." My friends have said "You're amazing! I can't imagine doing this!" They also say, "I wouldn't want to have a baby right now." Some comments are positive, and others not.

— Amanda, Ontario, Canada

. . . .

Your God-Given Role

> We can be the mothers our children need because God divinely chose us for the job. Don't doubt it. He knows what he is doing.
> — Elisa Morgan, president of MOPS International[3]

Faced with work and school responsibilities, most young moms don't have the luxury of staying home with their children. But even if your child is in the daily care of someone else for one hour or ten hours, you're still the mom.

Although you can never list "good mother" on a job resume, this role should not be diminished. Mothering isn't rewarded with a big paycheck or your name on the dean's list, but you're the only mother your child will have. Or as author Kate Douglas Wiggin put it, "Most of all the other beautiful things in life come by twos and threes, by dozens and hundreds. Plenty of roses, stars, sunsets, rainbows, brothers and sisters, aunts and cousins, but only one mother in the whole world."

God chose you to be that "one mother in the whole world" for your child. And if that doesn't show your importance, I don't know what does!

One cool thing about being "chosen" is that you were picked to be this child's mom for a reason. And while others can only see your exterior, God has a unique ability to see the heart. He can also see your potential to be a great mom!

. . . .

Positive Parenting

Another reason why your role is important is because the better mother you become, the better person your child will be for life.

As you may know, the first three years of a child's life are critical for the learning process. According to the American Academy of Pediatrics, "The ways in which parents interact with their children will set the stage for an infant's growth and development for life."[4]

This is the time when you, as a mom, play a huge part in deciding who your child will be in the future. Here are just a few key areas.

- The food you provide helps your child's body to grow strong.
- Your hugs, kisses, and kind words build your child's sense of worth.

- Your love shows him the importance of loving others.
- Interactive play shapes his physical and mental abilities.

What you provide during these early years is the foundation a life is built upon. Just as a skyscraper needs concrete and steel for stability, your child needs solid love and steadfast commitment.

To be a good mother you don't need a nice car, a huge house, or a successful career. You don't need access to expensive toys. What's needed most is *you*.

"Mothering isn't about tasks," says Cheri Fuller, author of *Being the Mom You're Meant to Be*. "It's about building a relationship that lasts a lifetime."

Did you catch that? What you do today will last a lifetime!

Changes in Your Life

We could go on all day about the importance of mothering in the life of a child, but have you considered how mothering has affected you?

Life as I See It

Having a baby pretty much grounded me. Before I had a baby I guess you could say I was a wild teen. I was rude, inconsiderate, not caring about anything. But when I had a baby, I realized I was going to have to grow up really fast. I needed to set an example.

— Diana, Washington

Becoming a mother has helped some young moms stop to consider what they want from life. It's helped them get on track.

Before I got pregnant, I didn't think much about my future. When I was in elementary school, I used to dream about life as an adult, but when high school rolled around "future thinking" took a back seat to "having fun today." What mattered most was who was playing in the football game Friday night, where the party was Saturday night, and what could I do so my hangover wouldn't give me away on Sunday morning.

Once I became pregnant, though, I realized that my plans for a good future were not only vital for me, they were also important for my child. My thought process changed. I now wondered, What should I do about schooling? What classes can I take at the community college to help me in a future career? What job would I enjoy that will still allow me to spend quality time with my son?

Right now, your major decisions may center on your schooling options. Or they may concern where you should work or live. No matter what choices you're facing, mothering provides an opportunity to become a better person. A better person for yourself. For your future. For your child.

Your Turn
4U2 Try 1

Have you ever felt scared and alone? Read the following poem and circle any of the feelings you've experienced. When you're finished, consider who or what has helped you overcome these feelings. Then consider how you can help other moms who might feel the same.

Yes, I Am Young

People staring
staring at me
I want to scream
scream, yes, i am young
yes, i can do it alone
i hate having to try so hard
so hard to fit in
why do you look at me that way

like i need your pity
i am strong
i am her mom
i am me
you can't take that away
you can't make me change
i don't need your acceptance
i don't need you to like me
but then why do i feel so alone?
why do i feel like i was left to die?
why don't you like me?
is it because i look young?
is it because you are afraid i will do a better job than you?
i don't want to feel alone anymore.

—one young mom[5]

4U2 Try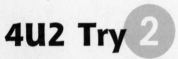

Moving Beyond Stereotypes

An attitude adjustment begins with you. Take a minute and quickly list some negative things you've heard, read, or thought about young parents. Across from each negative statement, write two positive statements to reflect your experience. Here's an example.

Stereotype	Reality
Young moms are too immature to raise a child.	Young parents have energy and know how to have fun!

4U2 Try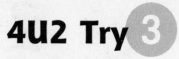

Messages for Baby

Check out the messages your baby needs most:

"I belong." Those hours in your arms give your baby the message, "I am loved. Somebody's there for me."

"I'm special." It is never too early to begin affirming your baby and letting him know how valuable he is in God's eyes and in your heart.

"I trust." Because in his distress you comfort him, your baby learns . . . that you will respond and are worthy of his trust.

"I can." Applaud your baby's milestones. Show your joy as he stretches his little body and his mind.[6]

Your Turn. Here's your assignment. Look at yourself in the mirror and tell yourself the same things you just told your baby. Finish these sentences:

"I belong because . . ."

"I'm special because . . ."

"I trust when . . ."

"I can . . ."

Live and Learn

My love today will mold my child's tomorrows!

2

who am I?
identity

People always say how you should be yourself, like yourself
is this definite thing, like a toaster or something.
                    — Angela, *My So-Called Life*

Charity staggered into Little Bear Daycare with Jackson on her
hip. He clung with chubby hands to her waitress uniform like
a baby monkey clinging to its mother.

"Here you go." Charity handed the diaper bag to the day-care
worker. "Oh man, I forgot his bottle in the car. I'll be right back."
Jackson squealed in protest as his mother handed him over.

"Love you, little guy." Charity kissed the outstretched hand that
reached for her, then sprinted to the car for the bottle. She couldn't
be late again.

Fifteen minutes later, Charity tied on her apron just as the minute
hand of the work clock struck the hour. Her boss cocked one eyebrow but didn't say a word. She'd made it—just barely.

Throughout the day Charity was happy to scoop up the spare
change she received from waiting on tables. While every penny of
her paycheck went to paying bills, she always put the loose change
aside for a special gift for her son. Charity had seen the red race-car
bed in the store window a few months ago and knew Jackson would

love it. At nine months, he already had a fascination with toy cars. She only hoped the tips would keep coming.

During her break, Charity hurried to her car to get the GED study guide. The big test was tomorrow, and she should have started studying weeks ago. As she hustled back into the restaurant, her reflection in the mirrored door stopped her. Charity looked closer. The girl in the mirror looked familiar, yet different somehow. With very little makeup, her hair in a ponytail, and ten extra baby pounds left to lose, Charity hardly resembled the girl she was a year ago.

"Miss Perfect," her school friends had called her. With a chic haircut, a great body, and a wardrobe to rival any sitcom star, Charity had been the envy of the girls in her class—and a catch for the guys. And one had caught her, all right. Caught her good.

"Now, look at me," Charity mumbled as she swung open the door. "I look like a frumpy, overworked mom . . . which is exactly what I am."

That image stayed on Charity's mind throughout the day. *Who have I become?* she asked herself more than once as she waited on customers. She was a student and a daughter—although those roles had changed dramatically. She was an employee too. And she was a mom. More than anything she felt that last role had overshadowed all the others, leaving little room for anything else.

While Charity knew she wouldn't trade her son for the world, she wondered, *Who am I? Is there any "me" left?*

Life as I See It

I'm learning by doing things as a mum, and I grow every time I do something for my son. It's hard to find my identity. Sometimes I don't feel like I'm growing up and other times I do.

—Sarah, Sydney, Australia

My life has changed so much since having my daughter. I can't do the things that I used to. I don't have half the friends I did before. I'm having to grow up faster than I should.

— Nina, Texas

· ·

I'm Not Sure Who I Am

> A miracle. A mystery to myself. Who am I? The mirror says back, "The George you was always meant to be." Wasn't always like that. Used to look in the mirror and cry me a river.
>
> — George Foreman, former heavyweight boxing champion

All of us moms—whether we've been a mom for a few days or a few years—ask ourselves the same question. "Who am I?" When our children enter the world, they not only have their own identity, but they *zap* ours as well. Suddenly we're not in charge of our lives. We're not even in charge of our minutes. We become diaper-changing, bottle-making, baby-rocking, sweet-talking mamas. Or at least that's what we do on the outside.

On the inside we're in limbo. We're young. We like doing all the teen things: seeing friends, having fun, hanging out, and shopping at the mall. But we often find ourselves friendless, fun-less, unavailable, and broke.

Did Ya Know?

One definition of *identity* is: "The set of characteristics by which a thing is recognizable or known."[1] What are you known for as a mother? As a friend? As a person?

As new mothers we often need help defining who we are. Does who we are depend on what we do? Does it depend on how we look, or what others think about us? The answer is no. *Who we are* goes deeper than that. It's our inner self that only we know. But discovering our identity isn't only a concern for young moms. Mothers of all ages and in all stages ask the same questions.

After the birth of her child, a mom moves from focusing on her personal needs, to being driven by the needs of a small human being. And although she may enjoy her new role (most of the time), like Charity, there are days she looks in the mirror and sees a stranger. A stranger she asks, "Who are you?"

Tricia's Blab

Listen Up

The day your baby is born you begin to discover who this new person is. In your child, a new identity is born. But on that day a second person is also birthed. A mom. Whether you like it or not, you're a different person than the one who began the labor process.

Pause and consider: In what ways are you different after becoming a mom?

Who Am I?

> I think I speak for everyone here when I say, "Huh?"
> — Buffy, *Buffy the Vampire Slayer*

Not too long ago when someone asked you to describe yourself, you may have defined it by something you were involved in.

"I'm a student."
"I'm a goalie in soccer."
"I'm a junior in high school."

Or you may have identified yourself with something you've accomplished.

"I'm a poet."
"I'm a pianist."
"I play flute in the marching band."

Or perhaps you referred to yourself in terms of a relationship:

"I'm Susan's daughter."
"I'm Rick's sister."
"I'm Jeff's girlfriend."

Like most young moms, when you discovered you were pregnant many of your roles changed. *We're talking dramatic changes*. One minute you're running track, and the next you're shopping for strollers. One day you're comfortable in your skin. The next day your body is swelling and stretching in all the wrong places. You may have attended college and worked two jobs last year, but after having your baby it's a *big* accomplishment to get showered and dressed before noon.

With so many adjustments concerning your body, lifestyle, and roles, you may feel as if you haven't *processed the changes*. You question the person you've become. You also wonder what part the "old" you plays in your new life.

Identity 1: My Needs

> Motherhood. If it was going to be easy, it never would
> have started with something called labor.
>
> — Old saying

Kids have needs. Moms meet needs.

Striving to meet needs is what mothering is about, right? Everyone talks about the importance of dads. (Yes, they are very important.) But instinctively mothers carry most of the load. Of course, if meeting kids' needs were the only ones you worried about, life might not be bad. But there are others with needs, too. Our husband or boyfriend. Our parents. Even our friends.

How do we balance the needs of others and our needs?

This is a challenge. Part of our identity *will always* involve meeting the needs of others. But to what extent? Are you known for giving and giving, without asking for help in return? Do you always put your plans on the back shelf when someone else calls with a need?

We have to realize that it's impossible to give constantly. Like a pitcher of water, to be poured out, we first need to be filled up.

I've struggled with this. For many years I made the needs of others my first priority. I cooked my son a second lunch, because he didn't like the first one I'd fixed. Or I agreed to baby-sit for a friend, so she could go out. While it's good to help others, there comes a time when we do so much that we crumble. In helping others, I sometimes hurt myself. I was cranky, tired, overwhelmed. Sure, my friends liked me always being available, but I yelled at my son and let myself fall apart.

We'll talk more about balance later in this book, but I want to make one point: You have to place priority on your needs, or no one else will. If you don't value yourself, you can be sure others will take advantage of you, whether you're eighteen or eighty!

Life as I See It

My life has changed dramatically. I no longer think about myself but only for my baby. She always comes first. I can't just get up and go anymore because there are always diapers, extra clothes, bottles, and toys that must go too. I can't even go to the bathroom anymore without her coming in and watching.

— Desiree, Texas

. . . .

Identity 2: My Looks

> I am me, and I don't know anyone else that is me. So I
> guess in that sense I'm the one and only, but not in any
> kind of egotistical way.
>
> — Elijah Wood, actor

Take a minute to think about the kids from high school. When I say jock, what image comes to mind? What about grunge, gothic, or nerdy? We all know that we choose our clothing to make a statement.

In our pre-pregnancy days we too had our own styles. Think back to your "look." What statement were you trying to make to the world?

For many of us, our fashion statements change after having a baby. (Today you may be sporting playing-in-the-sandbox shorts with a floral-print T-shirt to hide spit-up. Nice.) Instead of spending fifty dollars at American Eagle, there are diapers, formula, and wet wipes to buy. "Whether you want to accept it or not, you play a big part in the way other people respond to and treat you," says Jay McGraw, author of *Life Strategies for Teens*. "It all has to do with your behavior, particularly the way you present yourself to the world through your appearance, attitude, actions, and the way you treat others."[2]

What we choose to wear, and how we present ourselves, makes me think of Halloween costumes. I remember my favorite. In the third grade I decided to be Barbie. My mom bought one of those boxed costumes that had a plastic face with holes for eyes and a mouth-slit to breathe through. It also came with a shimmering pink "gown" that tied in back.

I thought I was beautiful . . . until my face started to sweat under the plastic. It was hard to see, not to mention breathe. I felt like I was suffocating.

After that Halloween, I never wore another plastic-mask costume. However, that didn't stop me from trying to be something I wasn't. It's easy to slip on a "mask." To hide behind a smiling façade. But attempting to be something I'm not doesn't feel good. Doesn't look right. And it's hard to breathe.

I'd like to say that as I grew older, I stopped hiding behind masks. But that wasn't the case. As a high school cheerleader, I always felt like the odd one out. Most of the other girls were a size 0 — and I was not. Needless to say, I was always the one on the bottom of the human pyramid! I tried to make up for not being super-thin by wearing all the right clothes and dating a handsome guy. I strove to be popular, and I went to parties even though I really didn't enjoy the atmosphere.

Years later, the masks were updated, but they were still there. After I had my kids, I attempted to be the perfect mom. For instance, I signed my son up for T-ball even though he didn't enjoy it. My three-year-old daughter took ballet, despite the fact that the class was a forty-five-minute drive each way and she couldn't have cared less about dancing. (She did like the tutu, though.)

When I took time to think about my identity, I started asking myself questions. What do I feel comfortable wearing? Where should I focus my time and attention? How would I like to be identified as a person?

I also reconsidered my motives. Why did I go to parties or watch movies that I didn't really care for? Why was I trying to be something I'm not?

Perhaps you can ask yourself the same questions. Taking time to evaluate your identity will help you fit life around *who you are inside*. Not the other way around. When you treat yourself as a valuable person, others will catch on. You're the one in control. It's up to you to decide how you want to be seen and known — without pretending to be something you're not.

Life as I See It

At first, I felt like I had disappointed everyone, and nothing would ever be the same. I thought everyone would look at me like a slut or something. I've learned that what other people think of me isn't as important as what I think of myself. I'll go somewhere now, and people will ask me about the baby—like they're excited and happy for me. I would have never expected that! It really makes me feel good.

— Katherine, Texas

Identity 3: What I Am Not

> Becoming a mother is a complicated thing. Not only am I trying to negotiate a relationship with my child, I am trying to negotiate a relationship with myself as I attempt to determine how I mother, how I feel about mothering, how I want to mother and how I wish I was mothered.
>
> — Andrea J. Buchanan, in *Mother Shock*[3]

Sometimes the easiest way to discover who we are is to know who we are not.

- *We are not our children.* We all know mothers who go overboard trying to make themselves look good by making their children look great. I saw one woman on the *Oprah* television show who had bought her preschool daughter more than twelve pairs of black shoes just so the girl could have different styles to go with her numerous outfits! Just as we don't get report cards for mothering, we also don't get graded on our child's looks or accomplishments. While you want your children to do their best and succeed in life, your self-esteem shouldn't be wrapped up in your child.

Life as I See It

My individuality will never end. There will be no one exactly like me, not even my child. She will be like me in some ways, but not at all in others. I wouldn't have it any other way.

— Desiree, Texas

- *We are not our mothers.* I remember the first time I heard my mother's voice coming out of my mouth. The words "because I told you so . . ." escaped before I had a chance to squelch them.

    It's not until we have kids that we truly understand our mothers—all their frets, their nagging, and their worries. It's also then that we truly understand their love.

    Since you are now a mother, it's good to think back on how you were raised. If there were traditions or habits that now seem wise and useful, incorporate them into your parenting. You also have permission to sift out things you now know weren't good. Just because you're a product of your mother, that doesn't mean you have to turn out just like her. Repeat after me, "I am not my mother."

- *We are not like any other mother out there.* Sometimes you may feel like the world's worst mother. After all, your friend never yells at her son—and sometimes you do. Then again, your friend may feel bad because you have a wonderful bedtime routine that includes stories and songs. In many cases, the moms you feel inferior to only *look* like they have it together. All moms feel they don't "measure up." Instead of feeling unworthy, we should realize that everyone has strengths and weaknesses. The key is where we place our focus.

    The Bible says, "Let's just go ahead and be what we were made to be, without . . . comparing ourselves with each other, or trying to be something we aren't" (Romans 12:5–6, MESSAGE).

The problem with comparison is, *we always measure our weaknesses against the strengths of others.* Instead, we need to thank God for our strengths. We can also ask God to help us overcome our weaknesses—not because we want to compare ourselves, or look good in someone else's eyes, but because we want to be the best mom out there.

Identity 4: I'm Not Who I Was

> I'm a firm believer in the power of change. But there's one thing I've learned . . . the hardest part of moving forward is not looking back.
>
> — Sally, *Felicity*

How different are you today from who you were before your pregnancy? Some moms still have a handle on their old selves. Others feel an ocean of difference separates the two. While it's okay to look back, here are two warnings:

1. *Don't dwell on your past identity,* believing your greatest achievements are behind you. Instead realize that having a child doesn't mean you have to kiss your dreams goodbye.

   I've learned this as I've followed the path to becoming a writer. It was after the birth of my son that I first considered writing for a living. The more I thought about it, the more I realized it made perfect sense. As a child, I loved to read. In middle school, my family lived by a library and I spent all my free time there.

   When it came to my identity, I could have moped over my past. I could have fretted over my choices. I could have clung to the pain of being abandoned by my old boyfriend. But instead,

I decided to look forward, not back. When my son napped or watched cartoons on Saturday mornings, I read books about writing and plunked away on the computer. I put my overactive imagination to good use, creating stories and magazine articles. It's then that I knew my greatest achievements were not in my rear view mirror. With hard work, I had plans for a great future.

2. *Don't base your identity on past mistakes.* Angela, a character in the TV series *My So-Called Life,* once said, "If life was like a giant VCR, our lives would be like videotapes. And we could fast forward past the really bad stuff and rewind the really good stuff. Except with my luck, I'd probably lose the remote and get stuck at, like, 'Cheerleader's Day' in the cafeteria."

   All of us at times wish we could rewind and change our mistakes. We can't, of course. Instead we can face our regrets in the following ways:

   a. *Seek to renew relationships with those you've hurt.* If you have an old friend you'd enjoy seeing again, call her up. If you've 'had words' with your mom or dad, try to make up. If you've cut other family members out of your life, spend time getting to know them again.

   b. *Work to overcome bad habits that get you into trouble.* You may hate the fact that you used to drink too much, or that you treated people with disrespect. Don't dwell on those regrets. Instead, make a doable plan to overcome bad habits that stick around like gum on the bottom of your shoe.

   c. *Consider your past failures as learning experiences for the future.* Regrets help us to change and make us want to do better. Sure you've messed up at one time or another. Everyone has. At least you know what *not* to do!

· ·

Identity 5: I Am Unique

> Nobody can be exactly like me. Sometimes even I have
> trouble doing it.
> — Tallulah Bankhead, early Hollywood star

We know we're not our children, not our moms, nor our friends.
We're not what we wear. We're not who we were. So . . . who are
we really?

One reason it's hard to figure out is because we're dealing with
something called personality. Personality is experienced and felt, but
it's hard to describe. Funny, quirky, quiet, and boisterous are all
words that can describe personality.

One fun thing that can help determine personality is those zany
"personality tests." Businesses use them for hiring. Dating services
use them for matchmaking.

CHECK IT OUT

Do you want to know a little more about yourself? Do
you also want to know the type of person you'd be compat-
ible with?

If you have internet access, check out these sites.

eHarmony: www.eharmony.com An on-line dating service that gives
you an in-depth personality profile. Then they match you with your
perfect "fit."

Queendom: http://www.queendom.com/tests/alltests.html#demo This
site has tons of tests. Make sure you look for the ones that say "free,"
otherwise they'll want to charge you!

- Did you discover anything new about yourself?
- Did any of these personality tests give you insight on your current
  relationships?

Yet, even if you took every personality test available, they still couldn't determine the real "you." You are much more than a statistic, a body, a mind, or a number. One reason personality is so hard to understand is because it's intertwined with your "spirit" or "soul." (And I'm not talking about the style of music.)

Personality is something we're born with. It's something God put in us from the get-go. It's also something that develops as we interact with those around us.

Your personality isn't the only thing that makes you unique. Your looks do too. Maybe you have your mother's eyes or your dad's nose. Your hair might be thick or thin. You may be big boned or tiny. And if you've ever watched those forensic science television shows, you know that you're *you* down to the smallest part. DNA evidence proves no two people are alike. Baby, you're an original.

And you've been original from day one—as I'm sure your mother has told you. Even as a baby you had a unique personality and look.

Perhaps your personality traits "shined" during your toddler and preschool years. (Can you say Drama Queen?) Then things just got more interesting from there.

Of course, all of these unique traits are not just random characteristics, thrown together for unknown reasons. To quote Mother Teresa, "How wonderful it is to think that we have all been created for a purpose! We have not come into the world to be a number; we have been created for a purpose, for great things: To love and be loved."

As I've said, I work with young moms every week and I'm here to say they're each unique. Some of these moms have a hard time talking in a group. Others have a hard time zipping their lips. Some moms are cheerful. Others are quiet and thoughtful. Some are forgetful, and then there are those who can tell me every detail of our last five meetings.

And even though they are all different, I think they're all special. But as much as I love them, there's someone who loves them even more.

In the book *What Every Mom Needs,* authors Elisa Morgan and Carol Kuykendall state, "Our true identity comes not from looking into horizontal mirrors—at reflections of ourselves or our mothers or our past—but looking up at God. As we gaze into his face, we begin to get a true picture of ourselves. He created us in his image."[4]

And just what does God think of you? Yes, *you.* If he wrote down his opinion of you (which he has), it might come out like this:

- I created her in her mother's womb.[5]
- I delight in her.[6]
- She has stolen my heart.[7]
- I love her.[8]

Now is that cool, or what?

Tricia's Blab
Listen up

Everywhere you look there seems to be a new personality "test," such as:

"What Breed of Dog Are You?"

"What Is Your Emotional Age?"

"What Is Your Body Language Telling Him?"

And my favorite . . .

"Are You Sure You're You?" (Explanation: What separates reality from a dream? In the information age, there's no way to be sure that your life isn't just a long simulation.)

My question: If we could take every personality test available, could we ever see ourselves as God sees us?

My answer: No way! We are more wonderful, more complex, than even we can figure out!

. . . .

Identity 6: I'm Not Perfect

> Use what talents you possess; the woods would be very
> silent if no birds sang except those that sang best.
> — Henry van Dyke, author

All of us wish to grasp perfection. We reach for it, strive for it. And we all fall flat on our faces. Someone once said, "No one is perfect. That's why pencils have erasers." I don't know about you, but I've worn away a few erasers in my lifetime.

Being perfect isn't possible here on earth. There may be people who expect you to be perfect. (Yeah, Mom.) But you've messed up enough to know there's no chance of that. God knows that too. In fact, the whole purpose of God's coming to earth — in Jesus — was to forgive all those troublesome imperfections. When we embrace this gift of forgiveness, our lives are changed. Our future is changed.

"This life was not intended to be the place of our perfection," says author Richard Baxter, "but the preparation for it." When we accept the gift of Jesus' sacrifice, we can look forward to a future with God — on earth and in heaven.

. . . .

Identity 7: I Am Loved

How many movies, books, and songs deal with the topic of love? Countless. In fact, there isn't a topic that's written about or sung about more often. Love is big business.

According to the Romance Writers of America, romance novels generated $1.5 billion in American sales in 2001 and have more than fifty million readers. That's a lot of love stories!

Have you had a difficult time with love? I have!

From the time I was in junior high, I was on the hunt for the perfect guy. I had a few crushes, but they didn't give me the time of day. Then one noticed me. He was more handsome, more wonderful, than I imagined . . . for the first two months. Then the perfect picture quickly got smudged around the edges.

What to do? I looked for someone else. Someone who would make me feel loved. I don't know why I expected total commitment from someone who wasn't old enough to shave, but I did!

It was an endless cycle. Meet someone, "go steady," break up. Once I got a little older, the relationships lasted longer — mainly because the physical element was added into the equation. But I soon found out that getting involved physically didn't help the chemistry. It just caused it to be more combustible!

At the time, I would have done anything for that true, everlasting, never-leave-you kinda love. I finally found it years later, but not in a boyfriend. I found it in Jesus — the one who loved me even when I didn't realize it.

In the Bible, John 3:16 says, "For God so loved the world that he gave his one and only Son, that whoever believes in him shall not perish but have eternal life."

While there are many religions that enforce "steps" to follow to become holy, there is only one religion that talks about a love you don't earn. When you accept Jesus as Lord, you don't sign up for a list of works. No preaching door to door. No shaving your head and wearing long robes. All you have to do is to *believe* in Jesus. Jesus who loves you as you.

When I fell in love with Jesus, it was then that I discovered my true identity. I found out that I'm special. I don't need to dress a certain way or try to be something I'm not. I could be myself, leave behind my regrets, and plan a good future. I didn't need to wear a Barbie mask. I was beautiful just as I was.

Your Turn

4U2 Try 1

Being Real

Read this exchange from *The Addams Family:*

> *Girl Scout:* Is this made from real lemons?
> *Wednesday:* Yes.
> *Girl Scout:* I only like all-natural foods and.beverages, organically grown, with no preservatives. Are you sure they're real lemons?
> *Pugsley:* Yes.
> *Girl Scout:* I'll tell you what. I'll buy a cup if you buy a box of my delicious Girl Scout cookies. Do we have a deal?
> *Wednesday:* Are they made from real Girl Scouts?[9]

If you had to describe the "real" you in fifty words or less, what would you say? For example, I came up with this:

> The real me is a mom who enjoys encouraging others, using the talents I was born with, and spending time with those I love and those who love me. I may seem like I have it all together, but the real me prays to God often because I feel weak.

Fifty words exactly! Go ahead, try it.

4U2 Try 2

Discovering the Unique Me

It's time for self-discovery. Read the following questions, and then write your responses. Don't answer with words that sound good, answers a friend, parent, husband, or boyfriend would like to hear. Answer how you *really* feel.

1. If you could choose one person (living or dead) to spend twenty-four hours with, who would it be? Why?
2. If you were given $10,000 and had to spend it in twenty-four hours, what would you buy?
3. If you could model your life after one person you know, who would it be? What qualities do you appreciate about this person?
4. If someone were to describe you, which qualities would you hope they mentioned?
5. If you could log all your thoughts for one day, what would you discover that you think about the most? Are these thoughts mainly positive or negative?
6. If you had a free baby-sitter for a whole day, what would you do? (Assume your house is clean and you don't need a nap!)
7. Alice Walker once wrote, "She wants to live for once. But doesn't know quite what that means. Wonders if she has ever done it. If she ever will." What does "to really live" mean to you?

4U2 Try 3

A quote from *The Wonder Years* says, "Change is never easy. You fight to hold on. You fight to let go."

1. What things in your life are you fighting to hold on to?
2. What things are you fighting to let go of?

4U2 Try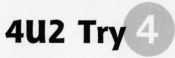

Identity

> My mother said to me, "If you become a soldier, you'll be a
> general; if you become a monk, you'll end up as the Pope."
> Instead, I became a painter and wound up as Picasso.
>
> — Pablo Picasso, artist

Think about it. How did your mother help mold your identity — both
for the positive and for the negative?

Now, how can you, as a mother, help your child mold his or her
identity? Write down three positive things you can do:

1.
2.
3.

4U2 Try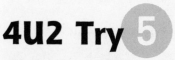

What's Your Label?

Did you know that food companies spend billions of dollars each year
marketing themselves to young people? M&M candies spends $67
million a year. Coke and Diet Coke spend $154 million.[10]

Does this advertising work? When I say, "Do the Dew," what do you
think of? What about "Just Do It!"

Your identity comes from who you are. Knowing that, think of a slogan
for yourself. Here are two examples: "Never Gives Up" and "Always
Sees the Bright Side of Life." What short phrase best describes you?

4U2 Try 6

Word Identity

Things Every Child Needs to Hear

I love you.

I'm so glad you came into my life. You have made it better.

There is no one just like you. You are special.

I adore your smile.

You fill up a special place in my heart.

My arms are always open to you.

You are smart.

You're extremely huggable.

I'll always protect you.

Don't be afraid. I am here.

You are my greatest treasure.

If all the children in the world lined up, I would still choose you.

Well done!

Things Every Young Mom Needs to Tell Herself

I am a lovely person.

I am unique and special.

I'm doing my best to be a good mom.

It's okay for me to dream.

All moms need a break.

I don't need to feel guilty when I take time for myself.

My good example will make all the difference in the world and to my child.

I become wise when I seek counsel from wise people.

It's good to hope for a better future for my child and myself.

Truth is always the best choice.

Life looks brighter when I focus on what's really important.

My habits will become my child's habits, so I better choose good ones.

What I have in the end will never mean as much as who I am.

There is no greater feeling than when my heart is at peace.

I don't need to worry about the future. I just need strength for this moment.

Well done!

Live and Learn

Knowing my identity means knowing my value
as a person and a mom.

3

where am I going?
growth

It takes a lot of courage to release the familiar and
seemingly secure, to embrace the new.
— Alan Cohen, author and
inspirational speaker

Jessie rose from her beach towel and stretched in the noonday
sun. The air was heavy and warm. She looked toward the lake
with longing.

"Go for a swim. You know you want to." Nick's voice was husky.
"I'll keep an eye on Tyler."

Jessie looked to her son. The baby lay sleeping on his belly in the
shade of the beach umbrella.

"Okay, I give in. I'll be back in a few." Jessie took mincing steps
toward the lake's shoreline, the sand hot as barbecue coals. The first
splash of water felt refreshing. And by the time she was knee-deep,
a full smile filled her face.

It's been too long. In the water, her body naturally took over as if
weeks, not years, had passed since she was on the swim team.

Stroke, stroke, breathe. Stroke, stroke, breathe. The familiar
movement came back as Jessie knew it would. Her arms and legs,
neck and shoulders worked in unison, until she was caught up in the
power of her strokes. The power she felt in the water.

I have to do this more often. I need this. The sounds of the shore-line faded behind her. Her worries, the stress of taking care of a child and of trying to keep peace with her boyfriend, slid away with each stroke. Soon only gliding through the water mattered.

After a few minutes, movement in her peripheral vision caught her attention. A white buoy bobbed up and down, announcing the end of the swimming area. Jessie reached for the thick rope connected to the buoy and turned toward shore. She'd gone farther than she thought. The people on the beach looked like ants on an anthill. Her coach's warnings about swimming alone ran through her head. It was too far to call for help if needed. Jessie's heart raced — not only from exertion but also from fear.

What am I doing? What if something happened to me? Who would care for Tyler?

As soon as she caught her breath, Jessie turned and headed back. This time her crawl stroke was labored, and she felt a tinge of pain creep up her side.

You can make it. She urged her body forward. *Don't forget you were offered a scholarship. You won meet after meet. You can make it back to shore . . .*

Finally, Jessie's foot scraped against the lake bottom. Breathing hard, she walked onto the beach. She pushed her wet hair back and looked for Nick and Tyler.

There. She spotted their umbrella, only Tyler wasn't under it; he was in Nick's arms. His back was arched and his screams bounced across the shore like a Frisbee. Nick was glaring toward her. As she hurried toward them, Jessie didn't know who was more upset — her baby or her boyfriend.

"Sorry about that." Jessie reached for Tyler. He instinctively quieted in her arms.

Nick swore under his breath. "I told you a short swim. What was that?" He kicked the sand, then turned away.

"I said I was sorry."

Nick sunk onto his towel, and Jessie sat on hers with Tyler on her lap.

That was so stupid.

Or was it? Even as she sat there, Jessie couldn't help but watch the other swimmers as they moved through the water. From age eight, her dream had always been to be a college swimmer. Now it seemed that dream would never come true.

Still, something told Jessie not to abandon her ambitions. Perhaps there could be another way to fulfill her longing. She wondered if even her small goals, such as lifeguarding or becoming a swim coach, were out of reach. Since Tyler came along, every small step seemed like a huge hurdle.

Someday, maybe?

- -

Life Lived on Hold

> We all learn by experience, but some of us have to go to summer school.
>
> — Peter DeVries, author[1]

Have you ever heard the sentiment, *When you hold that little baby in your arms, the whole world stands still?* In a way, that phrase is true. With a child there is no saying, "You can wait." There is no silencing the constant demands. There's no putting him away on a shelf, to bring down at a more convenient time.

Instead we use the shelf in other ways. That's where we stash our dreams, our plans, and our desires. It's the highest shelf. Out of reach.

Some young moms question if their dreams still make sense. When stacked up next to reality, dreams often seem foolish. Who cares about your desire to become a journalist when you have to put food on the table?

After becoming a mom, sometimes simple goals are all we can handle—making it to work on time or having the groceries last until payday. With feedings, naps, and diapers, who has time to dream?

Still, as noted earlier, a young mom longs to know her efforts are significant. She needs to feel that her mothering, and her life, matters. She also requires a sense of identity—knowing the person she is, and the person she's meant to be.

Life as I See It

I'm a stay-at-home mother at the moment, and I'm hoping to get a job in the next few months. It's overwhelming because no one wants to hire a teen mum, or young mum, around here. Some people even look at me weird, but I guess that's how it goes.

— Sarah, Sydney, Australia

I really don't think the programs set forth for us by government agencies are realistic. For example, when I started school I applied for the child-care expense credit. They denied me and noted, rather condescendingly, that they did not cover such programs as cosmetology.

— Travis, Michigan

The Need to Grow

> Twenty years from now you will be more disappointed by the things that you didn't do than by the ones you did do. So throw off the bowlines. Sail away from the safe harbor. Catch the trade winds in your sails. Explore. Dream. Discover.
>
> — Mark Twain, author

I once read, "Any dead fish can float downstream—it takes a live one to swim against the current."[2]

Though it's easy to let our dreams die and allow hopes to be swept away in the flow of a busy life, it doesn't feel right. Something in our hearts tells us there is more to life than minimum wage and TV reruns.

While we enjoy spending time with our children—giving them love and attention—we also want to do more, be more. We want to make a difference in our neighborhoods, our communities, and our world. We want our minds to think great thoughts. Our hands to create.

The history books are filled with ordinary people who accomplish *extra*ordinary things. There are also extraordinary people who do ordinary things. Such as the teacher who goes out of her way to see that inner-city kids excel. Or the musician whose favorite audience is her child. What you have to offer this world, big or small, is important!

Life as I See It

At the time I found out I was pregnant, I was collecting information to attend school in Washington D.C., specifically looking into the CIA. (I had been invited the year prior and spent a week on a tour checking into various job opportunities to finalize my decision.) Just thinking back on this makes me wonder . . .

— Marjie, Montana

. . . .

Growth Benefits Your Family

Being a mother, as far as I can tell, is a constantly evolving process of adapting to the needs of your child while also changing and growing as a person in your own right.
— Deborah Insel, author[3]

I once had a plaque hanging in my kitchen that said, *When Mama ain't happy, ain't nobody happy*. How true! Your attitude plays a big part in the "attitude" of your home. Those around you, especially your child, will pick up hints on how to act and react in this world.

If you've been a mother for any time at all, you've probably figured out that almost everything you do will be copied. A building block held to your child's ear becomes a phone. A toy car pointed toward the TV becomes a remote control. Your frequent expressions, such as *No!* or *Stop that*, will be repeated.

Also, consider the way you respond to things. When your child knocks over a glass of milk, you can either yell—or you can clean it up and tell her everyone makes mistakes. The situation doesn't change, but the outcome makes a big difference.

Our attitudes as moms improve when we have time for inward growth. When a mom has a chance to read a book or sketch a picture during a lazy afternoon, she'll feel better and her family will benefit.

Which means, as hard as it is, moms need time to dream, plan, and grow. While it may seem impossible (especially since you're balancing work, school, friends, family, and mothering), take a few minutes each day to think about (1) who you want to be, and (2) how you can get there. Allow your mind to wander as you take a shower or drift off to sleep. This "think time" will encourage inner growth that will benefit all areas of your life, especially your attitude toward your family.

Life as I See It

I haven't played my beloved guitar in over a year. And art? What art? As for other outlets, I'm pouring my juices into starting a club at school for other parent-students. I think it's a worthwhile cause, and I'm fighting for it.

—Amanda, Ontario, Canada

There's a story I read about Little Mary who was visiting her grandparents' farm. Investigating the chicken lot, she came upon a peacock. She ran quickly to the house, shouting, "Granny, come quick! One of your chickens is in bloom!"[4]

Perhaps today you feel like a chicken. Ordinary, plain. But, did you realize you're actually a peacock, waiting to bloom? Did you also realize this blooming will benefit your family?

Just as the small things are mimicked, your child will also copy how you pursue dreams. When she sees you learn new things and become excited about living, she will do the same.

In her book *Wishcraft,* Barbara Sher says, "The environment that creates winners is almost always made up of winners. . . . Their kids can observe, close up, how things really get done—not by magic, but *step by possible step.*"[5]

Growth Benefits Your World

> The measure of achievement is not winning awards.
> It's doing something that *you* appreciate, something you
> believe is worthwhile. I think of my strawberry soufflé.
> I did that at least twenty-eight times before I finally
> conquered it.
> — Julia Child, chef and television personality

Without a doubt, Wilbur and Orville Wright changed the world, manning the first air flight in 1903. (Not very long ago, when you consider how widespread flying is today.)

The Wright brothers grew up in a small Indiana town. Still, even when they were young, they were not afraid to try things out, to be curious. Orville once wrote, "We were lucky enough to grow up in an environment where there was always much encouragement to children to pursue intellectual interests; to investigate whatever aroused curiosity."[6]

You may not invent the next form of transportation (then again, you might!), but your contribution to the world *is* important. You can touch the lives of a few people or many. And you can start today.

One young mom I know is doing exactly that. Nikki had her first son, Jack, when she was seventeen, and her daughter, Kimberly, at nineteen. Nikki started attending our Teen MOPS group in Kalispell, Montana, when she was pregnant with her second child. The loving support Nikki experienced was exactly what she needed to bloom. With help from her mentor, and the other leaders, Nikki finished high school and grew more confident as a mom and a person. Now Nikki helps others as she was helped. She assists the leaders during the meetings by helping with the paperwork. She also introduces herself to new moms, offering encouragement and support. Nikki has discovered that when it comes to helping others, even little things like these are meaningful.

Anne Frank, known for her World War II diary, once wrote, "How wonderful it is that nobody need wait a single moment before starting to improve the world." If you're like Nikki and are looking for ways to improve the world today, here are some ideas to get you started.

1. Thank a friend who has helped you.
2. Make and take a card to someone who needs encouragement.
3. Wash another mom's car.
4. Spend ten minutes reading to your baby.
5. Offer to watch a friend's baby so she can pursue a dream.
6. Help a friend with her homework.
7. Bake a cake for someone you care about—just because.
8. Give a hug to someone who's encouraged you.
9. Introduce yourself to another young mom at the park or McDonald's.
10. Bring other young moms together and create a support group.

Your Growth Is a Gift to God

> Thank you for making me so wonderfully complex! It is
> amazing to think about. Your workmanship is marvelous
> . . . You were there while I was being formed . . . You saw
> me before I was born and scheduled each day of my life
> before I began to breathe.
>
> —Psalm 139:14–16 LB

This passage blows me away. Not only does God love me, he thinks I'm a work of art. He likes the way he made me. He had a plan for my life before I was even born.

Wizard of Oz star Judy Garland once said: "Always be a first rate version of yourself, rather than a second rate version of somebody else." In other words, don't attempt to be something you're not. Get excited about your uniqueness.

Dannah Gresh, author of *Secret Keeper,* puts it this way: "You were created as a masterpiece and *you* are one of God's expressions of beauty. Short, tall, thin, thick, freckles, big eyes, small ones . . . it doesn't matter."[7]

Thinking about God's purpose reminds me of the house plans I once drew in my high school drafting class. I sketched a design for an amazing, three-story house, with large pillars out front. The kitchen sparkled with enough elegance to host Julia Child's cooking show. The dining room sprawled big enough to hold the studio audience. But my favorite part of the blueprint was the tub in the master bathroom. I drew that thing big enough to sink up to my neck. Imagine that.

Instead of sketching a dream house, imagine your dream life. Think about each "room." Perhaps your "kitchen" is filled with those who you enjoy spending time with. Your "family room" can hold your most comfortable things. What makes you feel at ease, at rest? Maybe put those things in your "living room."

How about your "office"? What sparks your creativity and industriousness? What lights a fire under you and makes you want to accomplish big things? What is your "master bath"? What one thing most moves or excites you?

If you have trouble answering these questions, I have good news! For thousands of years, smart people from around the world have been asking about the meaning of life. The meaning of *their personal lives too.*

The Bible has had the answer all along. "It's in Christ that we find out who we are and what we're living for. Long before we first heard of Christ and got our hopes up, he had his eye on us, had designs on us for glorious living, part of the overall purpose he is working out in everything and everyone."[8]

Or to put it another way, "The easiest way to discover the purpose of an invention is to ask the creator of it," says Rick Warren, author of *The Purpose-Driven Life.* "The same is true for discovering your life's purpose: Ask God."

Don't tuck away the blueprint of your life in a dusty drawer. Living up to your potential is a gift—to yourself, to your family, and to the One who created you.

Growing Pains

I remember the first time my son realized he had grown. He was two and was knocked off his feet—literally. One month he'd been able to run under the dining room table with ease. The next month, his head connected with the hard wood, which sent him sprawling.

Perhaps you remember a similar growth spurt in your life. It was a time when your arms and legs stretched faster than you learned to use them. I remember as a child, waking up as my muscles and bones ached, attempting to stretch farther than was comfortable.

Then there were times when I was growing in all the wrong places, such as during pregnancy. T-shirts failed to cover my expanding abdomen, allowing my belly button to peek out. My jeans no longer fit. And my life didn't fit either.

Growing into a responsible parent can be painful too. College classes stretch us. Finding new friends makes us uncomfortable and awkward. And like a baby who needs to learn to duck his head, you have to understand that you're different than before. Growth means stretching your hours, your focus, and your abilities.

You may feel like you can't make it to the end of the day. Growth is learning to push through it. Do it anyway. Prove yourself.

Before you became a mom, finishing a term paper on time might not have been a big deal. Now it's a reason to be proud of yourself. Growth means meeting challenges you never thought you could face, whether they are graduating from high school, getting your driver's license, or finishing the art class you've dreamed about taking.

It also means making a commitment to yourself. *(Yes, I can do this.)* Growth means stepping out of your comfort zone and into your courage zone.

Life as I See It

After facing the idea that I was pregnant, my next obstacle was to get through my summer classes. I did an archaeological dig for weeks nine to fifteen of my pregnancy. It was rough because it was so hot and humid on the site, but I made it. Everyone was shocked that I had done that. They couldn't imagine working through morning sickness and the exhaustion of the dig. I felt like Superwoman for that.

— Amanda, Ontario, Canada

Moving at a Snail's Pace

> You must dare to dream, but there is no substitution for
> hard work . . . because no one gets there alone.
> — Dana Scully, *The X-Files*

Have you ever watched a flower grow? First, you see a tiny shoot. Then a bud begins to form. The green nub starts to open, and soon you see bits of color. Before you know it, the flower unfolds. It's perfectly formed, offering beauty and fragrance.

Yet growth in humans is much more complicated. Growth not only involves the body, but it also involves your mind, your emotions, and your spirit.

Physical growth is the easiest to see, especially in your child. Your baby may seem to grow like a weed (which grows twice as fast as flowers). But for yourself, you may question whether you're changing and improving at all. Like a 4x4 Monster Truck bogged down in the mud, you feel stuck. Worse yet, you're spinning your wheels with no progress.

I have a friend who measures her children's growth on a wall in their hallway. At least a dozen times I've watched her children flatten their backs against the wall to see if they've grown — sometimes more than once in a day! What adults realize, but kids may not, is that growth takes time. A yardstick or lines on the wall can't measure the internal growth we seek.

Costly Choices

> Far away there in the sunshine are my highest aspirations.
> I may not reach them, but I can look up and see their
> beauty, believe in them and try to follow where they lead.
> — Louisa May Alcott, author

Choice means cost. The choice to stay up late will cost you sleep. The choice to attend a night class at your local college costs money and time spent away from friends or family. The choice to take a walk in the park instead of cook dinner means peanut butter and jelly again. The same is true when we work on our internal growth—there's always a price tag. The question to ask is: *What will it cost to achieve my dreams?*

Perhaps you feel the cost of your dreams is too high for this moment in your life. Consider becoming a "taster." For example, you might not have the money to attend a fine art academy, but you could sign up for a pottery class at your local community college.

My friend, Jessica, has always dreamed of becoming a professional photographer. But with small kids at home she felt it was unrealistic to start her own business. Instead of forgetting about her dreams, Jessica uses her kids as models for practice. It's a picture-perfect opportunity! In the future she hopes to open her own studio, but until then Jessica focuses on improving her craft.

What do you dream about doing?

. . . .

There's a Dream in My Heart

> To accomplish great things, we must not only act, but also dream; not only plan, but also believe.
> —Anatole France, 1921 Nobel Prize winner

Dreaming can't be done well while you're changing dirty diapers or hurrying off to work. It takes getting away for a few minutes to let your mind wander. It means putting on a detective's hat (a la Nancy Drew) and looking for clues in your character.

When you were younger, as with most kids, you may have had a hard time deciding what you wanted to be when you "grew up." One day you wanted to be a teacher, the next day a lawyer. You still may question what you want. The key is concentrating on the one passion you find yourself returning to. What dream clings to you like a sweaty T-shirt no matter how you pull and tug?

Get out the magnifying glass and consider where you've been and where you're going. Sleuth around your home, your life, and consider what things are important to you. Is it caring for others, being artistic, or using your brain to solve problems?

Here are some questions to start:

- What do I enjoy doing?
- What qualities do I appreciate about myself?
- Do I like working with people or working alone?
- When I look back twenty years from now, what accomplishments will I be the most proud of?

Answering these questions will help you figure out what dreams are most important.

. . . .

Growing through Education

> I love school, too bad classes get in the way.
> — Zach, *Saved by the Bell*

A good education is one thing that many young moms dream about. Education helps us be smart, well-rounded people.

As a young parent, your education may have been one of the first things to suffer. Attending classes while raising a child is tough. I know.

I clearly remember staying up, after a long day of parenting, to work on math homework. I'd be sitting cross-legged on my bed while my son cooed and kicked next to me. Then there were the days when the baby-sitter cancelled, and I ended up taking my son to my college classes. Thankfully, my instructors were understanding and let us stay—although I don't think they appreciated that some students were more fascinated by Cory's coos than their lectures!

So where are you in your educational process? I know many young moms who have gone on to graduate from high school and college. The key is making a plan. So let's make one:

- Write down your three top educational needs.
- Write down three possible solutions for each need.

Example:

Need: To get my high school diploma or equivalent.
Options: Local high school, community college classes, GED[9] course, homeschool, and other alternative schools.

After you know your needs, and think of solutions, the next thing to do is make a plan of action.

. . . .

Your Plan of Action

> Excellence can be achieved if you risk more than others
> think is safe, love more than others think is wise, dream
> more than others think is practical, and expect more than
> others think is possible.
>
> —Anonymous

To dream is to plan. To dream big is to put that plan in writing and take small steps to achieve your goal. Many coaches and consultants use the acronym SMART to explain goal setting. SMART refers to goals that are Specific, Measurable, Achievable, Realistic, and Time framed.

Let's take a closer look:

- *Specific.* Pick a large goal. Is it finishing school? Finding a better paying job? Next, break that into *specific* smaller goals. Once you have your list, choose one thing you can accomplish this week.

- *Measurable.* Mark off your achievements as you complete them. The check marks on the page *prove* you're making progress.
- *Achievable.* Don't set yourself up for failure. Pick small goals you can complete in a short period of time. Then use the small goals as stepping-stones to the larger ones.
- *Realistic.* Be honest with yourself. How much time will you need to reach this goal? What talents will you have to develop? Are you willing to commit?
- *Time Framed.* Set time limits for your goals. Deadlines give a sense of urgency. You can do it!

Growth Involves Sharing Your Dream

Once you've settled on a plan, the best recipe for success is to find a partner to help keep you on track. Choose someone you trust and respect. Take time to share your goals with this person. But also be sure to listen to her goals. The key to an accountability partner is consistency. Try to talk at least once a week to discuss your progress and to spur each other on.

When I first desired to be a writer, I connected with another young mom named Cindy who had the same dream. Since I was often stuck home without a car, we spent time discussing our dreams over the phone. Because of our mutual encouragement, we've both seen our dreams become reality.

Remember that the best type of accountability partner is a friend—not your mother who will nag you or a counselor on whom you can dump all your problems. Look for someone who is encouraging and future-minded. Think about this friend as your personal, devoted fan. Someone to tell you that you *can* do it. Someone to be your dream keeper.

• •

Create Yourself

As a final thought, realize that to live as a mother is to live with change. Each day consists of moments of learning and growth. For our children, growth can be measured in inches and pounds, but as a mother, growth means choosing who we want to be and seeking God's help.

In the Bible, Proverbs 16:9 says, "In his heart a man plans his course, but the LORD determines his steps."

Your life is like a lump of clay, ready to be formed into something beautiful. The same God who placed your interests and dreams in you, can help you see them through.

Your Turn

4U2 Try 1

What Do You Tell Yourself?

The process that goes on in your brain throughout the day has been called "self-talk." One negative comment you tell yourself can undo dozens of positive ones in one fatal swoop. If you find yourself dealing with negative self-talk, here's how to cope:

The next time you feel yourself beginning to react emotionally to a situation or person, try the following activities recommended by Les Parrott and Neil Clark Warren, authors of *Love the Life You Live*.

1. Identify the situation.
2. Identify what you're saying to yourself about the situation through your self-talk.
   • Is it realistic?
   • Is it negative?
   • Is it self-condemning?

3. Take a deep breath. Face up to the reality and go with the flow. If you follow such a self-talk style, you'll gain a calm, a peace (instead of a headache) . . .[10]

Here's an example:

1. You find yourself on a date with a guy who turns out to be a real dud.
2. What do you tell yourself?
   - Is it realistic? Here's an unrealistic example: *Of course, I should have known this guy would be a loser.*
   - Is it negative? For instance: *What's my problem? I should have said no—I knew better.*
   - Is it self-condemning? *I'm so lame. Why didn't I just say no? Now I've wasted a whole evening.*

3. Take a deep breath, face up to the reality that you made a bad choice, and tell yourself you'll do better next time. We can't make perfect choices all the time!

Why is positive self-talk so important? Mainly, as the saying below relates, what you *think* determines how you live:

How do you control your destiny?

Watch your thoughts; they become words.
Watch your words; they become actions.
Watch your actions; they become habits.
Watch your habits; they become character.
Watch your character; it becomes your destiny.[11]

4U2 Try

Monitor Your Growth

> Talk is cheap. Words are plentiful. Deeds are precious.
> — H. Ross Perot, entrepreneur and
> former presidential candidate

Just like growth marks on the wall, you need to mark where you've been to see how much you've grown. In the process of change and exploration, consider using one or all of the following ideas to monitor your progress:

Journaling. Keep a notebook of your thoughts. Jot down the progress you're making in your growth and the various feelings you experience on your journey.

Mementos. My windowsill near my desk is cluttered with mementos — photos of special days, ticket stubs from events, small trinkets I've picked up during various trips. These are special reminders that I'm moving in the right direction.

Create a growth chart. Are you familiar with growth charts for infants? You can create your own growth chart for your goals. Use lined paper to keep track of days and months. Then record your progress. You can record character goals, such as going a week without using a curse word. Or personal goals such as checking the want ads for a new job. Mark down your progress, and then reward yourself. (Five small goals accomplished can equal one tall latte!)

4U2 Try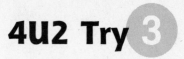

> How far you go in life depends on you being tender with the young, compassionate with the aged, sympathetic with the striving, and tolerant of the weak and strong. Because someday in life you will have been all of these.
> — George Washington Carver, inventor and educator

Growth means not only being concerned about yourself, but also thinking about and caring for others: the young, the aged, the weak . . .

- Get a piece of paper and draw a line representing your life to this point. Draw ups and downs to represent the high and low points in your life. Include stars to represent key moments.
- What have you learned from your experiences? What do you appreciate about the good moments? What have the problems, hurts, and trials taught you?
- How can you use your life lessons to help others? Be specific. Once you think of someone you can help, make a date on your calendar.

I've done this with my own life before, and it's been very helpful. In addition to using my past experiences to help other young moms, another key moment was caring for my grandfather. During his last months, I took the time to take interest in his life's stories, and I saw how much it meant to him. This made me realize the importance of listening.

What life lessons can you use to help others?

4U2 Try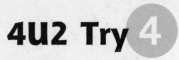

A Well-Balanced Life

Growth includes all areas of your being: body, mind, emotions, and spirit. How well are you taking care of yourself? Are you covering all the bases?

Body. Are you taking care of your body? Do you get enough rest? Do you exercise? Do you drink plenty of water? Are you making healthy choices? Are you choosing foods that fuel your body?

Mind. Are you giving your mind what it needs? Do you take time to explore your interests or to learn something new? Have you made time to read a good book? Do you take time to dream, and to share these dreams with a friend?

Emotions. Are you honest with yourself about your emotions? Do you share how you truly feel with someone who cares? Do you let yourself cry? Do you take time for fun?

Spirit. Do you take time to think about God and about what you mean to him? Do you pray? Do you spend time considering how the truths in the Bible affect your life?

4U2 Try 5

To Achieve Your Dreams, Remember Your ABC's

Avoid negative people and negative habits.

Believe in yourself.

Consider things from every angle.

Dream big!

Enjoy life today. Live in the moment.

Family and friends are hidden treasures. Seek them and enjoy their riches.

Give more than you planned to give.

Hang on tight to your dreams.

Ignore "dream destroyers."

Just do it!

Keep on trying. No matter how difficult it seems, it eventually gets better.

Love yourself. The most important opinion you have is the one you have of yourself.

Make it happen.

Never quit, lie, cheat or steal.

Open your eyes and see things as they really are.

Prepare and practice. Remember, it's perfect practice that makes perfect.

Quitters never win, and winners never quit!

Read, study, and learn about everything important in your life.

Surround yourself with "dream builders."

Take control of your own destiny.

Understand yourself in order to better understand others.

Visualize it.

Want it more than anything.

Xcellerate your efforts.

You are a unique creation of God. Live the life you have always imagined.

Zero in on your target, and go for it![12]

Live and Learn

Growing as a person will create a brighter future
for my child and myself.

4

do you love me?
intimacy

The body is a house of many windows: there we all sit,
showing ourselves and crying to the passers-by to come
and love us.

— Robert Louis Stevenson, poet

Carly twisted the key, then jiggled the knob to make sure the
door had locked. Eden babbled from her spot in the stroller,
her chubby hands pulling at her pink sunhat.

"No, you leave that on." Carly readjusted the hat over Eden's
blonde curls. "Want to go to the park? Leave it on, and we'll go to
park."

Eden clapped and pointed across the street. Carly approached the
street, looked both ways, and then pushed the stroller to Fairway
Park. This was her third visit this week. And since she didn't have
a car, she was thankful for a place close by in which Eden could get
some fresh air, romp around, and feed the ducks. It was also a great
place in which Carly could watch other parents and kids—which
was far more entertaining than any daytime talk show.

Eden squealed as Carly neared the kiddie area. Carly parked the
stroller by a miniature slide and tunnel and pulled Eden from the
seat. With wobbly steps the baby toddled toward the tunnel. Carly

laughed and shook her head, amazed that her ten-month-old daughter was already walking.

As Eden played inside the plastic tunnel, Carly noticed a couple passing by. A baby boy a little older than Eden was perched on the man's shoulders. One of the man's large hands was wrapped around the boy's two feet. The other hand was entwined with his wife's. The couple leaned close, as if sharing secrets, as they walked.

Baby Eden crawled to Carly and held up a rock.

"Thank you." Carly brushed her fingers through Eden's curls. The baby climbed back into the tunnel.

Two boys pedaled by on bicycles. Baseball mitts hung from their handlebars. A bat poked out of one boy's backpack. A pair of women speed-walked by in the other direction, their arms pumping in unison. Their laughter fluttered on the warm wind. Carly glanced away as they looked her direction. Feeling their gaze upon her, she reached for her daughter and repositioned the hat, proving she was an attentive mother. When they'd passed, she sighed and looked back toward the trail.

If only I had someone to talk to, to laugh with like that. More than that, she longed for someone special—a boyfriend or a husband she could walk along with, so absorbed in each other that the outside world dimmed in comparison.

I shouldn't do this to myself. Life was turning out better than she'd imagined. Her dad had helped her get her own apartment. She had a beautiful daughter and was studying to take her GED test. Family members stopped by once in a while and a few old friends did too.

Still, something was missing. Or someone. A heart-friend. A partner. Someone who would listen to her dreams, her troubles, and even that day-to-day stuff that came up as a mother.

Eden rubbed her eyes, and Carly checked her watch. Yup, it was that time already. Time for a snack and a long nap. Carly rose to leave, lifting Eden from the tunnel. Her daughter let out a shriek, realizing their time in the park was coming to an end.

"Nap time?" a voice behind Carly asked.

Carly turned and noticed another young mom approaching, pushing two toddlers in a double stroller. The woman had to be about Carly's age, and if Carly guessed right, the children looked like twins.

"Yes, a nap for me." Carly smiled as Eden wiggled and cried in her arms. "And hopefully one for her, too."

The other mom chuckled. "I remember hating naps, but now I live for them."

Carly buckled Eden in her stroller and turned to leave.

"Have a good nap, and maybe I'll see you here again," the other mom said.

"That would be nice," Carly called back over her shoulder. "Maybe tomorrow."

The other mom nodded. Carly smiled to herself during the rest of the walk home. The woman was a total stranger, but Carly noticed something in her gaze—understanding.

Eden's cries escalated as they reached the apartment. Carly sighed. She hoped that they *would* see each other again tomorrow, and maybe even the day after that.

. . . .

A Craving for Belonging

> We're all lonely for something we don't know we're lonely for. How else to explain the curious feeling that goes around like missing somebody we've never even met?
> — David Foster Wallace, novelist

I remember the last few days of my pregnancy. I was lonely and bored. It was like waiting in a long line at the fair. The line for this Ferris wheel seemed to move twice as slowly.

When I mentioned my boredom to a friend who had kids she laughed. "Once you become a mom, that will change," she said. "You may have days when you'll be lonely, but you'll never be bored."

I soon discovered my friend was right. In my new role as a mother there was no time to be bored. Loneliness was served up in abundance, though, along with a side dish of isolation.

Life as I See It

I sometimes struggle with isolation. I've tried desperately to find a group for mums and babies. At the same time, I started going to the gym and have made friends there. I've met some girls on the bus on the way to the gym, and a couple of friends make sure they call me . . . but it just feels lonely sometimes.

— Amanda, Ontario, Canada

I feel the most lonely after I put my baby down for the night. I don't have him to grin at me. Sometimes it feels like I'm the only one in the world who's awake at 9 p.m.

— Amanda, Ontario, Canada

Feelings of isolation and loneliness are one of the biggest complaints from young moms. Overnight, it seems they go from having lives filled with all types of people — parents, friends, teachers, coaches — to the monotony of having only one companion all day. As much as you love your little one, the shock of not having adults to talk to for hours at a time can be overwhelming.

As a young mom-to-be's abdomen swells, her list of companions usually shrinks. Sometimes it's due to changing roles. Other times it's due to *changing hearts*. Life is altered. We don't connect as easily. We can't do the same things. And no matter how much we tell ourselves that this baby will not change us, we feel different inside.

Yet, as with every other person, we are born with an inward need to connect. Babies in crowded orphanages die from lack of touch. When we don't connect with others who love us, something inside of us dies too.

I know one young mom who was scorned by her family when she became pregnant. Her parents allowed her to live with them but offered little love or support. Her life became a series of disconnections—chores, caring for baby, work. Even though her boyfriend was physically abusive, she moved in with him. She was desperately unhappy, but to her the rocky relationship was better than isolation. And she's still in that difficult relationship to this day. This young mom needed to feel loved—at any cost.

We all do. It's how we were created.

The Bible discusses this human need within its first few pages. In Genesis, it talks about God filling the earth with an abundance of life: animals, birds, and fish. And it was good. Yet the man God created, Adam, was alone. And that was not good.

That's where Eve came in. She was a special creation, designed to meet a specific need. Eve was someone Adam could talk with, work with, live with, and love. But that's not the only place the Bible talks about the importance of a companion. Ecclesiastes 4:9–12 (LB) says: "Two can accomplish more than twice as much as one, for the results can be much better. If one falls, the other pulls him up; but if a man falls when he is alone, he's in trouble. Also, on a cold night, two under the same blanket gain warmth from each other, but how can one be warm alone? And one standing alone can be attacked and defeated, but two can stand back-to-back and conquer."

God knows all about this thing called loneliness. He created us to connect with others. He created us with the need to love and be loved.

Unfortunately, loneliness can be more of a problem for young mothers than it is for older moms.[1] Young moms, like Carly, feel isolated from their friends, who are busy with normal teen activities: school, sports, or hanging out at the mall. And often, with all the many changes, they have little energy or opportunity for new relationships with people who understand being a mom and a teen.

I can relate to feeling lonely. I remember sitting bored as I watched my son play on the lawn in front of our apartment complex. As I looked at the puffy white clouds that graced the summer sky, I thought of the days when my friend Dawn and I used to just sunbathe and talk. On our backs, we'd whisper and laugh. We'd flip to our stomachs and read magazines, pointing out cute outfits and hairstyles. But we were older now, and we lived 1,000 miles apart. I missed her, and I wondered if I'd ever have another friend like that.

Just then another young mom walked by with her daughter. I dared to call a hello. She smiled and approached. Our kids played together that day and many days to follow. I'd found a new friend.

Making friends means reaching out. Here are places to start.

- Neighborhood parks, such as where Carly took her daughter.
- Fitness clubs, which sometimes have classes for mothers and their children; the YMCA offers "well-baby" classes at a low cost.
- Local coffee shops where mothers gather.
- More energetic moms speedwalk and push their strollers along bike paths.
- Local libraries, which often offer a "story hour."
- Churches. This is one of the best places to find moms. Many churches have programs targeted for young mothers, such as MOPS (Mothers of Preschoolers), often with free child care too!

Once you find friends, then it's time to nurture those relationships. But before we talk about how to foster intimacy, let's define intimacy in various relationships.

All about Intimacy

> The easiest kind of relationship for me is with ten thousand people. The hardest is with one.
>
> — Joan Baez, folk singer

What do you think of when you hear the word intimacy? Often, it is used as a nice way to say sex. Such as, *we were intimate last night*. While this is one definition, the kind of intimacy we're talking about is more than hugs and kisses, touching and intercourse. Here's how Webster's dictionary defines it: "The state of being intimate; close familiarity or association; nearness in friendship."

Life as I See It

What's intimacy? I live with my parents-in-law, and my husband won't even sleep in the same bed with me. Intimacy ends up being a morning kiss.

— Amanda, Ontario, Canada

Intimacy is something that is shared between two people. Something special like a good book or secret, and not necessarily sex.

— Desiree, Texas

Intimacy means having someone who you can confide in and trust. Someone who is always there for you.

— Jessica, Florida

Intimacy may mean holding hands with that special guy, knowing you don't need to speak. Or it can be those times when a husband and wife share their bodies in ways they will never share with anyone else.

Sometimes we feel the most intimate when at our worst. A friend of mine, Marie, became sick and was hospitalized soon after she started dating a man. Even though they'd only known each other a few weeks, he came to visit her in the hospital every night—just to sit beside her while she slept. He also took care of her cats and even washed her laundry. It wasn't the most romantic way to begin a relationship (for sure!), but the kind way he comforted Marie, helped her, and accepted her at her worst created an intimacy that a dozen candlelight dinners couldn't touch. They eventually married.

Friendships can also be one of the best settings for intimacy. Sometimes you just need someone to gab with about the stuff that guys just don't think about (such as makeup, good books, stretch marks, and labor stories!). A good friend will listen to your struggles and successes. And she understands when you *don't* want to talk, preferring to just hang out.

A loving family can be another source of intimacy. After all, who else can jump on your little brother's bed to wake him up? Who else knows how your mom likes her coffee?

Intimacy does not, should not, happen with only one person. No one person is able to meet all our needs. Our friends provide a different type of support than a husband or boyfriend does. If we expect another person to provide all the love and friendship we need, we're usually in for a rude awakening.

Here's another popular definition of intimacy: "Into-me-see." When we are intimate with someone, it's as if we're handing that person spy goggles to look into our souls. It also means looking into the soul of another. Intimacy is a two-way street, so if you want a clear view of another person, you must first offer a glimpse of yourself.

But building an intimate relationship is not something that happens overnight. "Intimacy—genuine intimacy—is not immediate. We expect it to be. The world around us tells us it is," says Elisa Morgan, author of *God's Words of Life for Moms*. "Singles walk into bars and come out as couples. Acquaintances share statistics about kids' ages and skills and assume they've connected."[2]

Elisa Morgan makes a good point: *Intimacy takes time*. It takes commitment—not giving up easily and believing in the other person. In our society it's easier to throw away than recycle, but recycling a friendship means searching for what's good and focusing on that.

Intimacy also means working to understand others and striving to be understood. It's not trying to change another person or having that person try to change you. Intimacy involves risk.

. . . .

Intimacy Obstacle 1: Time and Energy

> It's supposed to be hard! If it wasn't hard, everyone would do it. The hard, is what makes it great!
> — Jimmy Dugan, *A League of Their Own*

When it comes to friendships with other moms, the two most important ingredients for intimacy are *time* and *energy*. Fortunately, you have these in abundance, right? Wrong.

With numerous responsibilities filling your day, often the last thing you have time for is girl-time with friends. (And if by some crazy miracle you do have free time, often your first choice is sleep, or laundry!)

"What I really wanted to talk about with other new moms were the things I didn't hear anyone really talking about. I wanted to know if mothering was difficult for them too, whether everyone else had the same doubts or if it was challenging only for me," says Andrea J. Buchanan, author of *Mother Shock*. "We talk about our babies' physical progress, how they are beginning to roll or starting to raise their heads. We talk about losing pregnancy weight. We talk about feeding and diapering. I am so hungry for contact with people who understand the daily routine of life with a new baby that this almost suffices."[3]

Sometimes moms are also too tired to set aside quality time with a husband or boyfriend. It seems the guy in our life is the last one in line to get attention. (Which is not a good thing when he is supposed to be your partner.) Quality time with him can be, should be, spent in many different ways: having fun, talking, sharing dreams and values, and planning for the future.

. . . .

Intimacy Obstacle 2: Finding Good Friends

> If you build relationships on trust, you can trust the
> relationships you build.
> — Dorothy Madden, author[4]

Many young moms have a hard time transitioning between old friends and new ones. Friends their age are involved with "teen" stuff. Older moms are at a different stage in their lives—focusing on husbands, house payments, SUVs, and friends their own ages.

I remember how uncomfortable I felt attending Lamaze classes during my pregnancy, with my mother as my "coach." Everyone else was with a spouse, and while they chatted about decorating nurseries and taking maternity leave, I felt left out.

It's a rare treasure to find someone who can understand your unique role as a young mom. Someone who is facing the same challenges, and who enjoys the same things.

Life as I See It

I don't have someone I can really talk to. My husband and I live with his parents, and I feel like I can't talk to him because I should be grateful that we have a place to live. I am, but it seems like they want to run my life. I just want out of here! Then I can talk to my husband again and things will get easier.

— Amanda, Ontario, Canada

I have my friends and my sister to unload on. They are always easy to vent to because they usually have something to vent about too.

— Jamie, Montana

When looking for good friends the emphasis must be on "good." This can be a problem for those who have a habit of falling into unhealthy relationships.

We lose our objectivity in picking friends for different reasons. One reason is that we're needy. We *need* someone to like us, and if he or she is breathing, that's good enough.

Then there's the "fear factor." Afraid of being alone, we wonder, *What if this is the only person who will love me?*

Fear especially plays a part when we're looking for a relationship with a guy. We think Venom the Snake Boy is the best we can get, so we take it.

Another reason we may not choose good, dependable friends is that we have no idea what a healthy relationship looks like. Perhaps you've had negative role models, and you find yourself picking the same type of creepy guys or co-dependent friends that your mom or sister hung out with.

It's time to break the cycle. How?

1. One way may be to step back from your romantic relationship for a moment and take a closer look. Is your boyfriend trust-worthy? Is he loving? If your best friend were dating someone exactly like him, would you approve?

2. Ask yourself why you choose the type of men that you do. Is it because of the examples of others? Is it because you don't think you can get anyone better?

3. If you were able to do it all over, would you choose this person (either boyfriend or friend) to be in your life today? If not, why are you choosing to keep this person there?

I know it may be difficult. Evaluating your relationships may mean taking risks and stepping outside your insecurities. Remember, you are the example now. The positive relationships you model will make a huge difference in the type of people your child will choose.

Life as I See It

Hugs and Kisses are big in our home. I don't want our children growing up without affection. Whether it is story-time, play-time, or cuddle time we find time to let each member of our little family Know we love them. After all, children don't stay little forever.

— Marjie, Montana

Intimacy Obstacle 3: Deepening Friendships

> Those who bring sunshine to the lives of others cannot keep it from themselves.
>
> — James M. Barrie, author[5]

For some of us the problem may be nurturing our good friendships to the next level. Listen to David Duchovny, an actor in the TV series, *The X-Files:* "The key is to get to know people and trust them to be who they are. Instead, we trust them to be who we want them to be, and when they're not, we cry."

Do you have difficulty investing in friends?

"A toadstool can pop up overnight," says Elisa Morgan. "An oak tree, on the other hand, takes years to mature to full size . . . toadstool friendships don't require much investment. We camp on common ground, enjoy the instant intimacy that arises and then when it's gone, move on to another spot. But oak tree friends grow only with a greater investment. Time, availability, vulnerability, risk, spontaneity—these are the ingredients that fertilize an oak tree friendship."[6]

Have you taken time to understand someone for who they truly are, and not simply for who you wish them to be? Have others treated you the same?

Once you learn to accept each other, then it comes down to:

1. spending time with your friend,
2. listening,
3. helping your friend where she needs it,
4. and offering a glimpse of yourself . . . in order to take your friendships to the next level.

Intimacy Obstacle 4: Realizing You are Worthy of a Loving, Committed Partner

"I'll never have any suitors," said Meg.

"You don't need scores of suitors. Only one, if he is the right one," answered Amy, setting her straight.
— From *Little Women* by Louisa May Alcott

What qualities were you looking for when you hooked up with your baby's father? Was he the guy you always dreamed of?

I have a friend, Lynette, who made a list of all the qualities she was looking for in a husband. Some of the things she included in her list were confidence, kindness, and a tender heart. She was also looking for someone who would be her best friend, laugh easy, and treat her like a lady. Lynette set her standards high. Because she was looking with those things in mind, she found (and married) that type of guy.

I know of someone else who also had high standards for her future mate. A young woman named Ruth once wrote in her diary, "If I marry, he must be so tall that when he is on his knees, he reaches all the way to heaven. His lips must be broad enough to bear a smile, firm enough to say no, and tender enough to kiss. He must be big enough to be gentle and great enough to be thoughtful. His arms must be strong enough to carry a little child."[7]

The author of these words was Ruth Bell Graham, the wife of the most famous evangelist of all time, Billy Graham. And while no relationship is ever perfect (even this one), setting your standards high will bring a person into your life who you can live with and love for a lifetime.

When I hear stories like Lynette's and Ruth's I think, *If only I had the wisdom of these ladies!* In high school, I admit my top two criteria were: (1) good looks, and (2) thinks I look good. Yet having higher standards would have saved me a lot of heartache.

What qualities are you looking for? What would you place on your list?

Another question to ask is: What qualities do you have to offer?

We all want a great guy, but do we have the qualities to attract one? If not, which qualities do you need to work on? What is one thing that you can focus on that will make *you* the right type of partner?

CHECK IT OUT

I'm just saying, you know, you can't know who that person is, the person who will become your ultimate confidant. Your soul mate or your lover. He may be someone you've had your eye on for years, or he might be that guy standing next to you in torn jeans buying some part for his car. Whoever it is, he starts off as a stranger, so, it could be anyone.

— Sally, *Felicity*

Of course, sometimes it's hard to realize that you *are* worthy of a loving, committed partner. It's also hard to stop and consider what type of partner is best for you, especially when the world places more emphasis on "looks" than on "heart."

One example of this is what the media, especially magazines, tells young girls about the opposite sex.

Check this out . . . a recent issue of *Cosmogirl* (a magazine targeted for young teens) included these articles.[8]

"What Do Guys Like about You?"
"Ice Breakers (Wait for Guys to Come to You? Use These Lines and Take Control of the Conversation)"
"How to Be Well Liked"
"True Love Stories"
"Eye Candy" (a foldout of hot, half-naked guys)

The same types of articles were also found in the magazine *Girl's Life,* which focuses on girls age ten to fifteen. (That's starting in the fifth grade!)

Also, young readers can't turn a page without finding photos of sexy, thin, *older* models. *Girl's Life* also included "Summer Love" (how to discover what type of guy catches your eye), "Blind Dates," Q&A's about boyfriends, photos of the best bikinis, and a "health" page about being on the Pill.

The messages in these magazines for young girls are obvious: Winning a boyfriend is crucial, so you need to dress skimpy, approach guys boldly, and don't think twice about going all the way!

Yet what does that mean in real life? It may mean broken hearts and bad reputations. It may mean unplanned pregnancies or sexually transmitted diseases. One statistic even states that unmarried, teenage girls who are sexually active are three times more likely to be depressed than girls who are not sexually active! Also, girls who are sexually active are almost three times more likely to attempt suicide than are girls who are not active.[9]

Perhaps it's time to take a closer look at the "free love" messages media is telling young women, you and me included.

· ·

There's More to Intimacy than Sex

One main reason why young people choose to have sex is their desperate search for intimacy. But true intimacy is usually the last thing they find. Sexually active girls seek a lasting commitment, but end up with heartbreak.

Another side effect of the search for intimacy through sex is that these teens have a hard time learning other ways to relate. They miss the joy of heart bonds because society has fed them a lie that physical bonding is the only way to truly connect.

Think about it, in today's movies how do you know if two people are "in love"? *They have sex with each other.* While this may be an easy way to show attraction on the big screen, this isn't the real world. True intimacy is made possible by the use of relationship skills and *not* as a result of sex drives.

Tricia's Blab
Listen Up

I know I had the wrong ideas about intimacy when I was young. I thought that "going all the way" was the only way to show a guy that I truly loved him. And I wasn't the only one with this wrong idea! In fact, a new study on teen sex has shocked the nation. About 20 percent of twelve- to fourteen-year-olds have reportedly engaged in sexual intercourse before their fifteenth birthday.[10]

Think back.

What type of messages about attracting guys, getting guys, and having sex did you receive?

How did these messages affect you?

Did you feel you weren't "complete" without a boyfriend?

What do you wish you would have known about guys and sex at those ages?

Me too!

I often see young moms making the same mistakes I made. They are looking for love, and sometimes they make decisions and choose boyfriends based on what is easiest at the moment. A young mom may think, *Here's a guy who likes me. He likes my kid too. He may not be exactly what I'm looking for, but he's a whole lot better than nothing.*

Some young moms are willing to compromise because the guy fills their need for companionship. But, have you ever heard the saying, "Don't shop when you're hungry"? The same can be said about dating. Don't "shop" when you have an inner hunger that is desperate for a relationship. Otherwise you may end up with pork rinds when what you really need is a nice T-bone steak!

My advice to young moms who are looking for a companion is this: Wait for someone special who is better than just "good enough." Out there, somewhere, is a guy who is your "best." You are beautiful enough and smart enough to get the attention of many men. But don't waste your time trying different ones on like someone searching for the perfect bathing suit. Instead, look for, dream of, and wait for that special person.

CHECK IT OUT

"The owner of a photographic studio tells the story of a college boy who came in with a framed picture of his girlfriend. He wanted the picture duplicated. In removing the photograph from the frame, the studio owner noticed the inscription on the back, written by the girlfriend: 'My dearest Tommy: I love you with all my heart. I love you more and more each day. I will love you forever and ever. I am yours for all eternity.' It was signed 'Dianne' and contained a P.S.: 'If we should ever break up, I want this picture back.'"[11]

Too often when it comes to relationships, we're blind to what's obvious to those around us. A bad "pick" is easier to see in someone else's relationship than in our own. We easily notice the faults in our friend's boyfriend, but we are blind to the faults in our guy.

After a bad breakup, young moms often find themselves saying, "I should have listened to my mom . . . or my friend. They could see what he was like all along."

"Whenever the truth is threatening, we tend to *reach for the blinders,*" says Jo-Ellen Dimitrius, author of *Reading People*.[12] It's time to take off those blinders and take a good look. Who are you choosing to commit to? Can he be considered your "best"? If not, why are you settling for less?

If you are currently in a dating relationship, again ask yourself how you would view your boyfriend if you were an outsider looking in. Are you sticking around because you're *needy?* Because of *fear?* The people with the biggest needs or fears are usually the ones that fill their lives with the biggest Mr. Wrong.

Also, our judgment in relationships disappears when sex is thrown into the mixture. Once the powerful and pleasurable ingredient of sex is added we tend to overlook even basic flaws . . . until the passion subsides, of course. But by then it can be too late. By then, your emotions are knotted tight.

Life as I See It

I hope I don't appear silly or boy-crazy, but it really would be nice to get out of the house and spend time with a date, feeling like I'm attractive and funny. It's like "Mission Impossible" though. I meet interesting guys. We laugh, and they ask what I do. I mention that I'm a mama and this glazed look comes over their eyes. As they politely make an excuse to leave, I can't help but hear the lyrics, "Another One Bites the Dust," going through my head.

— Leanne

. . . .

Where to Find Intimacy

The first duty of love is to listen.
— Paul Tillich, theologian

We know now that intimacy is connecting on different levels with good friends or a good partner. Still, where do we find it? Intimacy can happen in a park as you talk with a friend. It can happen in your marriage or committed relationship when you take time to listen and respect each other. It can also happen in a support group such as Teen MOPS — where you meet with other like-minded moms.

One relationship that isn't designed to meet your need for intimacy is that one you have with your child. Our children will always be a part of our hearts, but they are not there to meet our needs. I've often heard young moms say that they decided to have a child so they'd have "someone to love me." Children do love you (most of the time), but they shouldn't have to grow up under the pressure of making you happy.

. . . .

Marriage

If you are married, your husband should be your main source of intimacy. Of course, even married partners have different views of what intimacy means. One partner might think of intimacy as physical closeness (such as sex), while the other partner considers intimacy as being understood. In another case, one partner might show love by buying gifts, while the other person shows love by washing the dishes.

Here's one good way to learn each other's "love languages." Sit down with your partner in a quiet place and answer these questions.

1. I feel loved when you . . .
2. One thing you did this week that made me feel loved was . . .

You may be surprised by the answers!

Other problems with finding intimacy in marriage involves:

Making Time for Each Other

Married couples often feel they are heading in opposite directions, especially if they have different work and school schedules. In our home, my husband heads to work at 7:30 every morning, and I work from home. While I'm always eager to get busy on the computer, I find the mornings before he leaves are a good time for connecting. We talk as we eat our cereal. (What? Did you expect me to cook breakfast?) We also pray a one-minute prayer together, and I wave from the window when he drives away.

It sounds like the perfect arrangement, right? Let me assure you, this has been a work-in-progress. It all started when I took the time to think of one thing I could do to make time for my husband. (Getting out of bed was a good start.) Then, each of these other things was added over time.

Here are some other things we do.

- Greet each other. Whenever one of us arrives home, we take time to kiss and catch up about the day's events.
- Have movie time after the kids go to bed. It's great to snuggle on the couch together.
- Go to bed at the same time. I'm an early person and my husband is a night owl. We compromise by going to bed together about 10:30 p.m. (This is when the next level of intimacy begins!)

Unrealistic Expectations

If two words ever hurt intimacy, *unrealistic expectations* are it. I'll be the first to admit that this was my major struggle when we got married!

As you know, I had some bad relationships in the past, so when I found John who was loving, dedicated, trustworthy, and handsome, I thought I'd found the perfect guy. We had a quick engagement, and we were married nine months after our first date!

While dating, John and I spent a lot of time talking—so I thought I knew him pretty well. I also saw what kind of lifestyle he led. John worked hard at his job and at home. His house was always neat, and he even ironed his own clothes. (See why I thought he was perfect?)

Needless to say, when we got married, I had unrealistic expectations. We'd never talked about it, but I assumed that since he always cleaned and did laundry for himself, he would do it for all of us. Wrong!

And that was only one of our issues. I could spend all day discussing things like where to go at Christmas, how to spend money, how to discipline our kids . . . the list is long.

But in the end, it all comes down to communication and compromise. Years later, we still work on these things. I have my opinion. He has his. But talking through our issues, without getting upset, has helped us to unite in our marriage. It has also fostered our intimacy, because the more time we spend talking through problems and coming to compromises, the closer we become. And isn't that what intimacy is all about?

Life as I See It

My fiancé is great. He encourages me to grow and be confident in what I'm doing. He tells me how I'm a great mom, and he makes sure that I know I'm doing a great job.

— Amanda, Ontario, Canada

. . . .

To Have a Friend, Be a Friend

> When you dream alone, with your eyes shut, asleep, that
> dream is an illusion. But when we dream together, sharing
> the same dream, awake and with our eyes wide open, then
> that dream becomes reality!
>
> —Anonymous[13]

Do you remember your first "best friend"? Mine was Heather. We attended church together and played during the week. Heather's mom worked in a furniture store, and we would play "orphanage," pretending to lay imaginary children down for naps in the display beds.

As Heather and I got older, we attended different schools and went our different ways. Partings are a way of life. Yet as each of us grow, we learn to appreciate more fully the various friends that cross our paths.

"Not every friend is meant to be our best friend," say Elisa Morgan and Carol Kuykendall, "and not every friendship is meant to be forever."[14] Still, each of us hopes to find a friend who will be just that.

Here are five things to look for in a friend. Can you think of five more?

1. Trust
2. Honesty
3. Common interests
4. A positive outlook
5. A sense of humor
6.
7.
8.
9.
10.

One final thing to remember is that even with all your friendships combined, people can not be expected to meet every need. Just as God created the first man and woman with a need for each other, he also created them with a need for himself.

Henri Nouwen once wrote, "No friend or lover, no husband or wife, no community or commune will be able to put to rest our deepest cravings for unity and wholeness."

Some people may consider God as a far-off ruler who put people on this world, then left them up to their own devices. This couldn't be further from the truth. My favorite Scripture verse is Zephaniah 3:17, "The LORD your God is with you, he is mighty to save. He will take great delight in you, he will quiet you with his love, he will rejoice over you with singing."

I love this verse because it speaks of a God who is near. Who likes me. Who is able to calm me when I'm afraid. Who sings over me from his place in heaven. Now that's a friend I can appreciate!

Your Turn

4U2 Try ①

Springboards to Deeper Conversation

Do you want to get to know a new friend better, but you don't know where to start? Here are some conversation starters.

1. What is the happiest thing that has ever happened to you?
2. What has been the hardest experience of your life?
3. What are your secret ambitions, your goals for your life?
4. What are your deepest fears?
5. What about me do you appreciate the most?
6. What people do you most admire?[15]

4U2 Try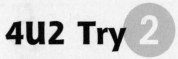

Eighteen Attributes to Look for in a Marriage Partner

Looking for Mr. Right? Think about the qualities you desire in a mate. Write them down. Here are a few to get you started.

1. Positive attitude
2. Spiritual values
3. Sense of humor
4. Faithfulness
5. Honesty
6. Respect
7. Good communication skills
8. Hard working
9. Compassionate
10. Playful
11. Generous
12. Forgiving
13. Flexible
14. Confident
15. Sensitive
16. Understanding
17. Common sense
18. Money-wise

— Al Gray and Alice Gray,
in Lists to Live By for Everything That Really Matters[16]

Live and Learn

I was created to love and be loved.

5

how do I do
this mom thing?

instruction

> Motherhood is like Albania — you can't trust the
> descriptions in the books, you have to go there.
> — Marni Jackson, author of *The Mother Zone*

As soon as she heard the scream, Jasmine knew she hadn't been watching her two-year-old, Quin, as closely as she should have. Sure enough she turned just in time to see Quin release his grip on the other child's arm. The girl's cries grew louder as Quin lunged for her again, his wild hands reaching for the flashing toy she clung to.

"Quin, no!" Jasmine jumped from the couch. She'd been invited to the support group for moms her age and things had been going well—for the first five minutes.

She pried Quin away from the girl. In typical Quin-style, he kicked his feet and yanked against Jasmine's grip.

"Mine!" Quin's strength amazed Jasmine. All other noise in the room ceased as moms and kids looked their direction. Even Quin's victim stopped her crying to watch the power struggle.

Some first impression, Jasmine thought. *They probably won't invite me back.*

"Quin, please! That's not your toy," Jasmine begged. "You have to share, okay?" This was her latest strategy to temper Quin's behavior — pleading. Unfortunately it worked no better than the yelling or time-outs she'd tried.

Jasmine dug through the toy box and found a garish-looking toy with music and lights. Quin calmed down and the noise in the room resumed as the other moms picked up their conversations where they'd left off.

Jasmine's cheeks felt hot. She wondered if she should just leave. After all, it would most likely happen again. She didn't want to go through another of Quin's "moments" in front of the other moms. Despite the various bits of advice she received from her mom, her neighbor, the pediatrician, nothing seemed to work . . . and things were getting worse. The bigger Quin got, the harder he fought against any type of discipline.

More than anything, Jasmine longed for step-by-step directions to raise a well-behaved child. She was tired of feeling like her son was controlling her more than she was controlling him. There were too many variables to this parenting thing. She needed to know:

- To spank or not to spank.
- When to stand firm, and when to let Quin make his own choices.
- What things she needed to teach at what time.

And that was just the beginning! It didn't help that each "expert" had different advice.

What's a Mother to Do?

Your teen years have been filled with learning and test taking. Your history teacher lectured on the American Revolution, and then you were tested on dates and facts. To get your driver's license, you learned the rules of the road and then took a driving test. But when it comes to this motherhood thing, there are no lectures (except, perhaps, from your dad). There's no instructor in your passenger seat, making sure you follow the rules of the road.

"People said to me when I was pregnant, 'Oh, your life is going to change!' as if they were not stating the obvious. My life had already changed—I was pregnant," says Andrea J. Buchanan, author of *Mother Shock*. "I knew to expect sleepless nights; I knew to expect crying; I knew to expect exhaustion; I even knew to expect joy. I didn't know to expect ambivalence. I didn't know to expect doubt."[1]

Mothers-to-be and new moms often overflow with doubt and questions. There's so much to learn about babies. There's the basic stuff, such as breastfeeding, burping, and when to introduce solid foods. But beyond the early survival skills, over the ensuing days and months, there are questions that arise daily. *How do I get my child to sleep through the night . . . to stop throwing his food on the floor . . . to mind?*

Whether you're still tackling the basic skills of mothering or seeking advice on more complex issues such as growth, personality, and development, the questions never end. So where can mothers turn for instruction?

Life as I See It

Overwhelmed by the responsibility of having to make all the decisions, having to provide for my son and plan for the future with no instruction manual to refer to. I feel frustrated because I have such high ideals as to what kind of mother I want to be but I can't seem to live up to them.

— Simone, New Zealand

I am certainly not saying raising children is a piece of cake, because it isn't. But support is so important. Insight and advice

from others, whether your parents, friends, neighbors, etc. They help so much to keep us from being stuck on one idea.
— Marjie, Montana

Basic Instincts

> Suddenly I was in unfamiliar territory. I'd had nine months to anticipate being a mother, and then about thirty seconds to snap into being one.
> — Andrea J. Buchanan, author of *Mother Shock*[2]

I remember those first few moments after my son was born. He was slimy, pink . . . and beautiful. I instinctively reached for him and held him to my chest, wanting nothing more than to give this child everything.

Mothering instinct is something that may surprise a new mom, especially one who hasn't had much experience with babies. Sometimes mothering instincts kick in from the start, and you know what your baby's cry means or something tells you to seek a second opinion concerning your child's health. Mothering instinct is an inner nudge that won't go away.

But mothering instinct shouldn't be thought of as some big, mystical change that transforms you the moment you give birth. Instead, it's more like a natural tendency to love and protect your child.

"Tough to prove and easy to dismiss . . . maternal instinct is a place where a mom must learn to trust her heart in response to her child," says Elisa Morgan, author of *What Every Mom Needs*.

That's not to say that every mom has mothering instinct. We've all heard those horror stories of women leaving their children in dumpsters. Some moms also suffer postpartum depression which, without help, can make them consider running away or hurting their child—things they'd typically never dream of doing.

For most of us though, when we see that squishy baby and breathe in that "baby smell," we begin loving and nurturing in ways we never thought possible. Even those who've never considered themselves a "baby person," find themselves suddenly changed when dealing with their own child.

Life as I See It

I am nineteen, and I have a fifteen-month-old little girl. My husband and I are expecting another. I often get looks or comments. Yes, I am young, I am married, and I have a daughter. Yes, she does sign language and she wears cloth diapers. And, yes, we are having another one. It just goes to show that the old saying is true. "Don't judge a book by its cover."

— Leanne

What really bothers me is when people say, "Wow, your daughter is really smart . . . you raised her?" Like a young mama can't have a smart baby.

— Tricia

Learning about Mothering

> When love and skill work together, expect a masterpiece.
> — John Ruskin, artist

A hundred years ago it was common for families to live near each other, with the older mothers training the younger ones. Today, families are often spread across the country. Even if they live close, experienced family members may be unable to provide hands-on help. That's why today's mothers look to different sources for advice, including parenting books, classes, and even internet chat groups—the new "community." Wherever you look for advice, it's helpful to focus on one issue at a time.

What do you need to know most urgently about your mothering today? Stephen Covey, in his book *Seven Habits of Highly Effective People,* believes that effective people "begin with the end in mind." They know where they're headed, so they "take care to get there." *Do you have an end in mind when it comes to your most urgent needs?*

This will help you know what type of advice to seek out. If your end is good health, you'll seek information on nutrition, sleep, and exercise. If your goal is "smarts," you'll incorporate reading aloud and other mind-stimulating activities. If your goal is a "happy, peaceful toddler," you'll seek information on how to control your schedule and your temper, applaud every success, and to have fun with baby. (No small task!)

Richer Than Gold

You may have tangible wealth untold;
Caskets of jewels and coffers of gold.
Richer than I you can never be—
I had a mother who read to me.
—Strickland Gillian (1849–1954)

Expert Advice

When I first became pregnant, I craved not only spicy chicken sandwiches and fries but also information. I realized that one Bible class and a childhood of eavesdropping on my mom and her friends wasn't going to cut it in terms of preparing me for the reality of childbirth and parenthood.
—Andrea J. Buchanan, *Mother Shock*[3]

Amazon.com lists 24,291 parenting books on their website. That's a lot of expert advice! Now the question is, where do you turn for *good* advice from trustworthy sources?

Doctors and nurses can be a good place to turn to. I know one young mom who was struggling to nurse her son. She thought she had to figure it out herself. She mentioned it in passing to her doctor, and the doctor sat down with her until she had the baby latched on and gulping. She's since learned doctors and nurses are happy to help with almost any parenting question. When you can't get in to see someone in person (such as over the weekend), you can seek out nurse hotlines, which are cropping up more and more. Check your local hospital or insurance company to see if they offer this service.

Other good places to search for advice are magazines and books, or radio and television programs. Here are some pointers for knowing which resources to trust.

- *Shop around.* Just because someone has an M.D. or a Ph.D. behind his name doesn't mean his advice is right for you.
- *Get referrals from friends.* If you see parents with well-behaved children, ask them for their favorite books and resources.
- *Consider more than one resource.* Read books and magazines and pick out what works for you. Choose the best and don't bother with the rest.
- *Consider your current needs.* As your child grows, your parenting style may need to change. What worked at twelve months, may not work at twenty months.
- *Listen to your heart.* Remember that no one parenting style works for every person. What is your heart telling you?
- *Seek help before a bad habit forms.* Kids know how to "work" mommy. For instance, they'll throw a terrible tantrum in the store, knowing Mom has to give in. The next time that happens, how are you going to handle it? Ask knowledgeable mothers on the best way to deal with situations such as this.

. . . .

Unsolicited Advice

Sometimes you look for advice, and, like it or not, at other times advice finds you. If you feed your baby a bottle, someone will advise you to breastfeed. If you breastfeed, you'll hear that your baby isn't getting enough milk, and you should offer a bottle. You'll hear well-meaning phrases like these.

"Use disposable diapers."
"Use cloth diapers."
"Let him cry."
"Pick him up."
"Rock him."
"Drive him around the block until he falls asleep."

The list is endless.

"Everyone, it seemed, had an opinion that I needed to hear, and often everyone's opinion was different," says Andrea Buchanan. " 'Take it from me,' people would say. Or, 'Let me tell you,' they'd begin. Whatever they said would always end with some piece of vital information that would doom me to eternal bad parenthood if I ignored it."

What do you do when others insist on telling you what *they* think? You can:

1. Ignore it.
2. Appreciate it.
3. Get irritated.

The best choice is a mix of numbers 1 and 2. Listen and be polite, but don't feel you have to follow their suggestions. (I agree that's hard to do!)

Of course, when advice is given in a condemning way, it's challenging not to be annoyed. People are quick to stick labels to you and your child. But realize that in the end *you're* the parent, and what you think is what matters most.

· ·

Moral Instruction

> We choose which seed we will plant in the lives of our
> children: good or evil; kindness or rudeness; selflessness
> or selfishness; happiness or sorrow; love or hatred; life or
> death. One day, the seeds will come to fruition, whether or
> not we live to see the harvest.
>
> —Cecil O. Kemp Jr.[4]

Another thing that kicks in when you become a mother is your
natural tendency to share your values, faith, and beliefs with your
child. Inner convictions help you determine how to treat others.
Convictions also help with decision making.

Most of the time, the values you choose to communicate aren't
something you sit around and think about. Instead of writing out a
ten-step plan on how to teach love, you simply model it.

Life as I See It

*To me my son is what he sees, so I make sure I am a very
positive influence in his life.*

—Nancy, New York

Some values you got from your parents. Others you've seen mod-
eled in people you respect. Just like placing an original document on
a Xerox machine, moms soon discover their kids often turn out to
be miniature copies of themselves.

"Children are natural observers," says Emilie Barnes, author of
Time Began in a Garden. "In fact, I've found that children see so much
more than adults do, perhaps because they're closer to the ground,
perhaps because they look at the world through fresh eyes."

So what qualities do you want your child to pick up? Do you want
her to know she shouldn't judge people by their outward appearance? Do you want her to be respectful of other people's things and
ideas? Do you long for her to eat nutritiously and exercise, or love to

read, or keep a clean room? Then you must show her how it's done. Modeling these behaviors is a gift to your child.

. . . .

"Do as I Do"

Want to know something that's impossible? Sneezing with your eyes open. Something else impossible is raising a child under the concept, "Do as I say, not as I do."

For myself, I want my children to know God's love and to know that he speaks to us through the Bible. So from the time they were very young, I've made prayer and Bible reading a part of our everyday lives.

Knowing what's important to you will help determine what things to pass on. It means being true to your convictions even when it is difficult or inconvenient. It means not settling with what's easy, and instead pursuing what's right.

Qualities to Pass On to Your Children

Determination . . . "Stick with it, regardless."

Honesty . . . "Speak and live the truth—always."

Responsibility . . . "Be dependable, be trustworthy."

Thoughtfulness . . . "Think of others before yourself."

Confidentiality . . . "Don't tell secrets. Seal your lips."

Punctuality . . . "Be on time."

Self-control . . . "When under stress, stay calm."

Patience . . . "Fight irritability. Be willing to wait."

Purity . . . "Reject anything that lowers your standards."

Compassion . . . "When another hurts, feel it with him."

Diligence . . . "Work hard. Tough it out."

—Charles R. Swindoll, author of *Growing Strong in the Seasons of Life*[5]

· ·

Mothering Mentors

> No one is a light unto themselves, not even the sun.
> — Antonio Porchia, author[6]

Have you ever met a person and thought, "I want to be like that when I grow up"? When I first became a mother, I looked to a woman named Cheryl as an example. She was caring and spoke to her children with affection. She smiled often and didn't get upset easily.

Everyone needs someone to look up to. I've had women in my life whom I esteemed as mentors—whether they knew it or not. Mentoring is a fancy word for "example." It's a person who's hands-on in your life and sets an example.

There are various places to find mentors. Some moms find them when they join play groups or support groups. Others look in places of worship to find women of common interests or cultural backgrounds.

A mentor is someone who has been where you are going. She's faced the same struggles, experienced the same joys, and usually has good advice.

Mentoring is not a new concept. Even the Bible talks about this type of relationship. Titus 2:4–5 (MESSAGE) says, "By looking at [older women], the younger women will know how to love their husband and children, be virtuous and pure, keep a good house, be good wives."

Many times mentoring also moves past the outward stuff and unites hearts. And while it may seem like the younger mother reaps all the benefits, older mentors greatly enjoy the relationship too. So when you spot someone who may fit the role, don't be afraid to ask her to be your mentor. Offer to have her over for a soda and use the opportunity to listen to her stories and enjoy her company. She'll appreciate getting to know you in an intimate way and will cherish the joy of helping, as perhaps she was once helped.

. . . .
Baby Steps

One of the best things to learn from a mentor is how to grow your character.

"I am always doing that which I can not do, in order that I may learn how to do it," said the artist Pablo Picasso. This applies to character qualities such as patience, gentleness, and consideration too.

When you want to spruce up your body, you can exercise, get a new haircut, or put on makeup. Yet there's no foundation or mascara to make the inside shine. (Oh, how I wish there were!)

In my early parenting years, there were days when I couldn't tell if I was making *any* progress in my character growth. Especially the days when the money ran out, the baby was sick, or the neighbor was grumpy. It was then when I displayed character I *did not* want my child to copy.

Inside I wanted to follow the teachings of the Bible. I attempted to treat others as I wished to be treated. I longed to be thankful for all God has given me. Yet my growth reminded me of the game Mother-May-I. I took three baby steps forward and two giant leaps back.

It was helpful to continually look to positive role models and caring mentors for encouragement and inspiration—knowing if they could do it, with God's help, I could too.

Also, I have another mentor who is always able to provide guidance: Jesus Christ. I can read about his loving interaction with others in the Bible. A good place to start is in Matthew, Mark, Luke, and John, books named after the men who wrote them. You can't get a more perfect role model than Jesus!

. . . .
Finding a Mentor

Whatever you are, be a good one.

—Abraham Lincoln

Have you considered looking for a mentor? A role model? Some-one who's done what you dream about doing?

When you look for a female mentor, ask yourself the following questions:

- Who do I admire? Do I have an older friend, relative, or perhaps a leader in a Teen MOPS group that I'd enjoy spending more time with?
- Does this person have time to spend with me?
- What can this person teach me about life? Parenting? Following dreams? Will this person encourage my growth?
- Is this person a healthy role model? Is she honest? Truthful? Accepting? Supportive?
- Does this person take time to listen to my concerns? Can I open up to this person? Can this person be trusted with my confidence?

If you find someone, here are steps to setting up a mentoring relationship:

- Ask if she'd be interested in becoming a mentor.
- State what you're looking for.
- Take time to interact, to listen, and to care.
- Give as well as receive.

Once you find someone to build a relationship with, together you can decide on the specifics of your time together. It's up to each individual mentoring relationship to consider their needs and goals. Consider:

- How often do you want to meet?
- What types of things would each of you like to discuss?
- What level of commitment are you willing to give?
- What will you do when you meet? Talk and share feelings, hopes, and dreams? Go through a book together? Pray?

Peers

Since not everyone has a mentor in their lives, the most common place that mothers, young and old, get advice is from their friends. Moms ask questions and swap advice through long phone calls, short discussions in the grocery store, during work or at playtime.

For a more focused arrangement try looking for support and encouragement through a Teen MOPS group. To see if there is Teen MOPS in your area, check out: www.mops.org or call toll-free (800) 929-1287.

Other places to call are local hospitals, churches, or parenting organizations in your community. We all need someone who understands. Nothing feels better than to share your up-all-night-baby-wouldn't-stop-crying experience with someone who can sympathize.

Life as I See It

What I'm doing as a mom is important. I keep going! I keep struggling and striving to be better—a better mother, a stronger woman, and a better-educated student. Every day I try to be less of a statistic.

— Travis, Michigan

I can only do what I can. There will be times I'll be discouraged, but with my determination and personality I know I'll make it. I just want to be a good mother, and wife, and that'll take a lot of effort and work. Right now, I've just been looking at other mothers, reading books, talking to family, and getting as much "guidance" as I can.

— Katherine, Texas

I'm trying to pursue a bachelor's degree in something that makes me happy and will provide us with a comfortable living. I feel if I keep the fire going inside myself, a few sparks will fly my daughter's way and encourage her to never give up.

— Travis, Michigan

God, the Instructor

Still there are times, when not even peers are available to share your heart with. That's why it's good to know that there is one person who's always available. Jesus is not only there to listen, he's there to instruct you with his words of truth. Still wondering what to do, where to go, how to live? "Let God transform you inwardly by a complete change of mind. Then you will be able to know the will of God—what is good and what is pleasing to him and is perfect" Romans 12:2b (TEV).

And isn't that the *exact* type of instruction we're looking for—instruction that is complete, good, pleasing, and perfect? For that, go to God.

Your Turn

4U2 Try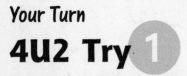

Wise Things Your Grandma Told You

Model these concepts for your child!

- You are special.
- Manners matter.
- Treat others the way you want to be treated.
- Your life can be what you want it to be.
- Take the days one day at a time.
- Always play fair.
- Count your blessings, not your troubles.
- Don't put limits on yourself.
- It's never too late.
- Put things back where you found them.
- Decisions are too important to leave to chance.
- Reach for the stars.

- Clean up after yourself.
- Nothing wastes more energy than worrying.
- The longer you carry a problem, the heavier it gets.
- Say "I'm sorry" when you've hurt someone.
- A little love goes a long way.
- Friendship is always a good investment.
- Don't take things too seriously.[7]

4U2 Try 2

There's been much good instruction passed down through the ages. Here are some keepers from *The Message*, in the book of Proverbs.

- "Better a bread crust shared in love than a slab of prime rib served in hate."[8]
- "Hot tempers start fights; a calm, cool spirit keeps the peace."[9]
- "Refuse good advice and watch your plans fail; take good counsel and watch them succeed."[10]
- "Put God in charge of your work, then what you've planned will take place."[11]
- "Friends love through all kinds of weather, and families stick together in all kinds of trouble."[12]
- "Answering before listening is both stupid and rude."[13]
- "Trust God from the bottom of your heart; don't try to figure out everything on your own."[14]
- "Listen for God's voice in everything you do, everywhere you go; he's the one who will keep you on track."[15]

4U2 Try 3

Helpful Advice

Are you tired of getting advice you didn't ask for? Here's some you might appreciate. In his book *Never Eat Anything That Moves*, Robert Bender gleaned the following advice from children. Here are some of my favorites:

- Never pull a cat's tail or the other end will bite you. *Brigham Shipley, age 10*
- If you can't find your gum, your shoe will find it for you. *Joslyn Smeal, age 11*
- One best friend is worth one hundred lukewarm ones. *Joseph Hyde, age 10*
- The worst advice I ever gave was when my brother asked me if B comes before A. I told him yes, but I wasn't paying attention. When he sang his BACs, it sounded awful. *Desi Casada, age 8*
- You're not in school to make friends. That's what detention is for. *Adriano Apostolico, age 12*
- If you get a bad grade on a test, tell your mom when she's on the phone. *Nichole Murphy, age 11*
- Never pick your nose when your mom slams on the brakes. *Lacey Shaffer, age 10*
- When you get mad, don't let your pain stay inside, you might break down. *Brittney Robinson, age 11*
- To sing louder, open your mouth and pretend there's an Oreo in it. *Dianna Vo, age 11*
- It's good to be young, because you will last longer. *Cara Iglady, age 7*[16]

4U2 Try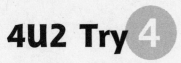

Instructions to think about . . . and live for:
- The six most important words: "I admit I made a mistake."
- The five most important words: "You did a good job."
- The four most important words: "What is your opinion?"
- The three most important words: "If you please."
- The two most important words: "Thank you."
- The one most important word: "We."
- The least important word: "I."[17]

4U2 Try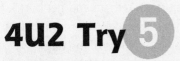

My Personal Favorite Advice
- Stick to your guns. If you tell your child to do something, follow through.
- Don't count. Teach your child to obey the first time.
- Don't let your child do at six months what you don't want her to do at two years.
- Don't let your baby use items as toys, such as phones or keys, that you wouldn't want them to play with when they get older.
- Don't teach your baby words that you'd hate for them to repeat in public. Swear words might sound cute coming from the mouth of a toddler, but they aren't cute coming from the mouth of a four-year-old.

4U2 Try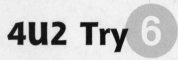

Communication is the Key to Obedience

When it comes to getting your child to obey, communication is key.
Here's how to get your toddler to listen to you and obey:

1. Get your child's attention. Make eye contact.
2. Tell her what you need her to do. Example: "Since you are finished playing with your blocks, Mommy wants you to put your blocks back in the bucket."
3. Give her the reason why. Example: "When you leave the blocks on the floor like that, someone can step on them and get hurt."
4. Give her the consequences. Example: "If you don't put the blocks away, I will have to take them away for the rest of the day."
5. If needed, give an alternative. Example: "I can help you pick them up if you ask me nicely."
6. Be consistent. Follow through with everything you've said. *This step is key.* If you "give in" your child learns that you don't stick by what you say.
7. Don't give in even if your child complains, whines, or cries. You want to reinforce good behavior. Giving in will reinforce that whining works!

Live and Learn

Seeking information helps me
to become an informed mom.

6

can you help?
help

There is no such thing as a self-made man. You will reach
your goals only with the help of others.
— George Shinn, owner of the New Orleans Hornets

Danielle unlocked the door, then pushed it open with her foot.
She set Alexis on the floor. The toddler squealed and ran
across the living room toward her toy box. Danielle slid her
backpack off and placed it on the table with a thud. She shut the door
and scanned the room. There was no sign of her husband, and . . .
she moaned at the sight of last night's dirty dishes still stacked in the
kitchen sink. She'd been up late studying for end-of-year exams, and
Damon had promised he would do the dishes today, his day off.

Where is he? She had counted on him to watch Alexis while she
cooked. *I'm going to kill him . . .*

Danielle glanced at the clock, realizing her new in-laws would be
arriving in less than thirty minutes. Alexis's squeals interrupted her
thoughts, followed by the crash of her plastic tea set being dumped
onto the floor.

"Ugh," Danielle pressed her fingers to her temples, then noticed
the note on the counter. *Hon, the boss called and needs me to come
in today. Promised overtime pay. Sorry about the dishes. See ya at
6:30.*

Danielle knew they could use the extra money, but six-thirty? Damon would get here the same time as his parents. How would she ever get dinner done, keep an eye on Alexis, *and* get the kitchen clean before her in-laws arrived?

Another crash erupted. This time building blocks tumbled onto the coffee table.

"Alexis no. Don't dump anything else—" Danielle's voice was cut off by a knock on the front door.

She froze, then felt her heartbeat quicken. *Please don't let them be early, please don't let them be early,* she pleaded as she approached the door. But as she looked through the peephole, she spotted the smiling faces of her in-laws.

I can't do this, Danielle thought, forcing herself to smile. *I'm going to go crazy if I don't get some help....*

. . . .

A Young Mom's Needs

What do you need most?

- More time to study.
- Help around the house.
- My boyfriend to live up to his responsibilities.
- A better job.
- Organization.
- My diploma.
- Money.
- Another me.
- Help!

Life as I See It

I need fun time with my little girl, communication with my husband, friends. Oh, and a bigger paycheck would help!

—Travis, Michigan

I need time to myself! My husband just doesn't get it. He's away at work and at play, all the time. My time-away is a half-hour at the gym. That's it ... except the dentist.

— Amanda, Ontario, Canada

Have you ever seen tags sewn into clothing that say something like this: "This garment is scientifically laundered to give the look of being old and worn. Flaws and imperfections are part of the total desired look."[1]

Do you ever feel old and worn? You've been pre-shrunk, stone-washed, and weathered. Flaws and imperfections pop up just when you think you've got a handle on things. The only difference is, this isn't your desired look!

Life as I See It

Most people I know do not have children and always invite me to places where kids just don't mix. Have you ever tried to find a babysitter on a Saturday night with only two hours' notice? It's like finding a must-have Christmas gift on Christmas Eve.

— Desiree, Texas

Each of us must deal with a reality check when our babies are born. Often when we do need help, we don't like to ask for it. (Or we don't know how to ask.) Sometimes we try to handle the challenges alone. Other times we *hint* about our needs. We complain about our workload to a co-worker. We moan about not getting enough sleep. We sigh as we do yet another load of laundry, secretly hoping that our husbands will pitch in. But playing the martyr doesn't work. So we complain, moan, and sigh even louder.

In the end, fear of failure drives us to push ourselves. We don't want to appear weak. We don't want our parents to say, *We knew you were too young for this responsibility.* And we don't want to think that of ourselves.

Another problem is that "it all" really needs to be done, and we worry that if we fall behind everything will fall apart. It's as if we're running a marathon at the pace of a sprint.

. . . .

Asking for Help

> And what is a man without energy?
> Nothing — nothing at all.
> — Mark Twain

I have a fatal flaw. I don't like asking for help. Even in high school, I would quietly study the chalkboard, attempting to figure out the jumble of math equations, instead of raising my hand to ask for assistance.

The same is true today. When a friend suggests getting our kids together to play, I volunteer to take her child. When someone calls and needs a meal delivered to a new mom, I accept the job. I like to give the appearance that I have it all together. The problem is that behind closed doors, I fall apart. I collapse onto my bed, with the many items on my to-do list swirling around in my head. I want to please everyone all the time . . . but it's just not possible.

There's another reason many of us don't seek help. While we may say we don't want to bother anyone, in truth we don't want to *owe* anyone. We feel uncomfortable about repaying another person's kindness. We don't like the feeling of outstanding debt. It's hard to ask for help. Really hard.

Or . . . we sometimes "save up" for help in case we *really* need it. We think, "I may need help more next week, so I'd better wait until I'm more desperate." Meanwhile we're pulling our hair out.

Life as I See It

I have a guilt trip about asking for help. I get that voice in my head that says I should be old enough, wise enough, mature enough, have it together enough, not to ask for help. I know that the voice in my head comes from my mother who made it quite clear through disappointed looks and lectures, that asking for help meant you failed.

— Travis, Michigan

Asking for help makes me feel weak. Yes, I have a hard time admitting I can't do it all. I don't want people to think I can't do it. Instead I want them to say, "Wow, what a good mom." I'm always worrying about what other people think of me as a parent ... it's not a good thing.

— Diana, Washington

Of course, there are some people who aren't fooled by our inability to do it all—our children. We may be able to keep up our appearance to the outside world, but the little ones with us day and night see what we're like under pressure.

"A volcano, in essence, is a natural thing that explodes under pressure," says Julie Ann Barnhill, author of *She's Gonna Blow*. "And that's exactly what can happen to us . . . In an instant we can change from the peaceful, nourishing women we want to be into Mount Momma—spitting fire and brimstone at all who cross our path."[2]

Trying to please everyone all the time doesn't work. We turn our lives, ourselves, into a frantic mess. In the end, it's our peace of mind—and our children—who suffer.

"There's no use trying to paste on a happy face or a good attitude to show in public if our hearts are cluttered with hidden issues," says Elisa Morgan. "What's stuffed down in our hearts will sooner or later spill over into our days with our children, our neighbors, our co-workers, and God."[3]

∙ ∙

Guy Help

> Authentic men aren't afraid to show affection, release their
> feelings, hug their children, cry when they're sad, admit it
> when they're wrong, and ask for help when they need it.
> — Charles Swindoll, author

When it comes to raising kids, the first person young moms should naturally turn to for help is a husband or the father of their child. After all, you're on this journey together.

As one young mom commented, "I think mums and dads share the same role in parenting because they are both parents and they have a child together."[4]

Some moms find great support from the man in their life. They are part of a relationship in which both partners work to love and support each other.

Life as I See It

My son's father supports me all the time. Sometimes it doesn't seem like it, but he is like a cheerleader who has lost his voice from cheering so much.

— Nancy, New York

My husband is always here for me. Through the blues after our first was born and the moodiness and tears with this second pregnancy, he is always there with a shoulder to cry on and a box of tissues. He never cared about the weight gain or the stretch marks, 'They're beautiful, you are having our babies' he says. He helps to tie my shoes or lets me know my socks are mismatched because I can't see my feet. I feel so fortunate that he loves me and our children and is not afraid to express that.

— Marjie, Montana

If you have a man in your life who has made a commitment to you and your child, there are things you *can* do to grow a relationship where both partners' needs are being met. Relationships take a lot of work, a lot of time, a lot of dedication. But when you work to build a special bond, all will benefit—you, him, and your baby. Here are some things you can do.

1. *Offer support and respect.* To get support and respect, you also need to give them. Think about your actions and words. Do they build up or tear down your partner? It's easy to be quick with the tongue and dish out criticism. It's harder to praise what we appreciate. It's easy to think of ourselves first. It's harder to think about the feelings and needs of others.

2. *Strengthen your relationship as a couple.* Relationships are challenging to any loving and committed couple. They are even more difficult between young people who face the numerous challenges of school, work, friends, raising a family—and the added task of growing up themselves. To make a relationship work, you need dedication and time spent together. You need to share your dreams, your feelings, and have a willingness to work toward a common future. You need to be able to communicate your needs and be willing to meet the needs of the other person. (Don't expect your partner to be able to read your mind!) Also, as Romans 13:8 says, "Don't run up debts, except for the huge debt of love you owe each other" (MESSAGE).

3. *Share the parenting load.* Sharing parenting responsibilities is tough, especially if the parents live in different households. One thing to do is develop a parenting plan. Sit down together and discuss roles and responsibilities. Discuss issues concerning your child's health, safety, and development. Decide who will do what when it comes to raising your child. Also talk about what you can do to support the other person's efforts.

Life as I See It

Right now my boyfriend and I are going through a rough time. He can sometimes be selfish and stubborn. He still wants to do what he wants, even if it's not the best for "the family." I just think that this whole thing about being a father hasn't hit him.

— Katherine, Texas

Me and my boyfriend are creating a relationship not just for us but for our son. We both understand that this is our child. We are both going to be in his life. Even if we hate each other sometimes, we make sure we don't argue or fight around him.

— Diana, Washington

My husband is a pretty good father, although as a couple we have a lot of communication problems. He was raised in a house where the adults didn't interact much with the kids. It's a struggle to explain to him that a two-year-old is not going to watch TV inside all day and still behave.

— Travis, Michigan

Lack of Guy Help

> Experience is a hard teacher: She gives the test first, the lessons afterward.
>
> — Anonymous

While many young dads freely give their care and support, there are at least an equal number of fathers who don't. Perhaps having a helpful, supportive partner is something you can only dream about. After all, as author Kent Nerburn states, "It is much easier to become a father than to be one."

Fatherhood is not a high school elective. Many young dads have no idea what being a parent is all about.

I once read a story about a group of people who were riding in a four-engine propeller airplane over Kansas when, all of a sudden, three of the engines conked out. Immediately the cabin door opened, and the pilot appeared with a parachute on his back. "Keep calm, folks, and don't panic!" he ordered. "I'm going for help."[5]

Perhaps your baby's father was like the pilot in this story—ditching you when you needed him most. Not only did you have to deal with the big "crash" of being all alone, you also had to face the sting of abandonment. (And boy, does it sting.) Then a new life arrives on the picture. How can you ever be mom and dad too?

Life as I See It

Sometimes I get really sad when I think that my daughter's going to grow up not knowing her father. Most moms have a husband behind them for the extra support and late nights, and even though my family tries, it just isn't the same.

— Jessica, Florida

The biggest challenge in raising a child is doing it alone—trying to raise myself and my son at the same time. Also going to college, working part time, and so much more.

— Diana, Washington

Right now I'm doing my best to do both jobs as a mother and a father. I know there are some things I can't do, so I compensate and do the best I can.

— Jessica, Florida

When it comes to single parenting, one common emotion young moms have to deal with is disappointment. When you raise your child without a father (whether by your choice or his), expect your feelings to fluctuate.

"Because the traditional American dream of husband, home, and family is so emphasized in our culture, you will be going through a normal grieving period over the loss of this dream," says Andrea Engber, author of *The Complete Single Mother*.[6] Expect yourself to get angry, to be upset. Allow yourself to grieve.

Another common emotion that young moms deal with is guilt. They feel it's their fault when there isn't a father involved. In some cases guilt is good. For example, *earned guilt* is another phrase for conscience. It's okay to feel guilty if you run a red light or copy a term paper off the internet. This type of guilt is an inhibitor. This guilt makes you think twice before you get yourself into trouble. It works to help you make better choices.

Unearned guilt is the unnecessary one. Perhaps you feel guilty because you can't afford your own place, or you can't buy your baby the same things a two-income family can provide. If you're feeling unearned guilt . . . stop! Let it go. Many young moms feel guilty they can't give their child a father figure. The guilt provides nothing productive. It just makes you feel worse about yourself. Unearned guilt can be axed when you realize you *are* trying to do the best for your child, and when you realize God can take your previous bad choices and turn them into good.

Handling Feelings about an Uninvolved Father

- Don't dwell on the idea that you are inadequate or that his rejection is due to a flaw in your character.
- Do think more about yourself right now and about your soon-to-be-child. Your responsibility is to yourself and not to the emotional issues your child's father is contending with.
- Do ask yourself: Is it single mothering I am afraid of or am I really upset over the father's reaction and possible departure?
- Don't try to counsel the father, help him cope, or apologize to him.
- Do accept responsibility for the decisions you are making now.
- Do acknowledge your feelings of regret or disappointment. Until you accept the reality of this loss, you are flirting with depression.[7]

Supporting Cast

> Some people can't believe in themselves until someone
> else believes in them first.
>
> — From *Good Will Hunting*

In the movie industry, actors and actresses that support the main star are known as the supporting cast. They are the ones who pop in at the right time, give their dialogue flawlessly, and make the lead actor look good. While it's true that you are ultimately responsible for your child, don't fool yourself into thinking you can do it alone. Every one needs a supporting cast.

Who do you have in your lineup? Maybe you have a special friend who doesn't care what your house looks like. Or a family member who thinks nothing of your old sweats and torn T-shirts. Perhaps you have a close companion who enjoys sharing leftovers with you and chatting about the day's events. Or maybe you have friends who enjoy hanging out and don't mind the noise of toddler tantrums.

Each of us needs someone we can turn to for advice, someone who can help us with child care or can give us a ride to the store. Your supporting cast is key to your success as a parent. A supporting cast is built one person, one relationship, at a time.

Think about your lineup of friends and family members. In movies, the main star may have one person who acts as a quirky sidekick and another who is the "mentor" character, dishing out wise advice.

Now it's your turn. Sizing up your lineup will provide you with a resource to turn to when you're looking for a little help. (Be sure to include their phone numbers for a reference!)

Who You Can Call When:

You need child care: _____

You need help with homework: _____

You're afraid: _____

Your child is sick: _____

You have an accident: _____

You want to exercise: _____

You need help around the house: _____

Your car breaks down: _____

You don't have money for rent: _____

You need legal advice: _____

You just want to have fun: _____

You are worried about your child: _____

You want spiritual advice: _____

Also, when you consider your supporting cast, think of it as a two-way street. Who can *you* support? Perhaps another young mom? Think about what you can do for her. Consider which of the above roles you can fill. When you practice reaching out, you will grow more comfortable with give-and-take. You will ask for help, because you've offered help. You will learn the joy of supporting each other.

Helping Each Other

I long to accomplish a great and noble task, but it is my chief duty to accomplish small tasks as if they were great and noble.

— Helen Keller, woman born blind and deaf[8]

In days past, families lived and worked in communities. Remember barn raisings in the *Little House on the Prairie* books and television show? The men worked to raise a barn, while the women provided the meal. The work was usually done in a day. The best part was the sense of togetherness.

I remember one time when I was attempting to clean up after a large gathering in my home. I was trying to be the "good host," allowing everyone else to relax while I cleaned. One friend insisted on helping.

"Two people do the work three times as fast," she claimed.

And you know what, it was true. The work was completed faster and was more fun when done with a friend. Another way to share the load is to share strengths—this can be referred to as bartering.

"Bartering makes it possible to spend more time on tasks you enjoy doing while allowing someone else to fill in on duties you don't enjoy as much," say Elisa Morgan and Carol Kuykendall, authors of *What Every Mom Needs*. Maybe you don't mind doing laundry, but you hate cooking, whereas your friend loves to cook. Swapping jobs can benefit both of you.

Find a friend to share the load with. Exchange baby-sitting. Work together on housework. Cook one meal and split it. There are many creative ways that you can get help . . . while giving it in return.

Life as I See It

My friend is the most caring person I know. We both have busy schedules, kids, work, and husbands. But whenever things are really good or really bad we always end up hugging each other!
— Travis, Michigan

Support Groups

> Cluster together like stars.
>
> — Henry Miller, writer

A *group* of helpful friends is even better than just one. That's why support groups help young moms in many ways.

"I take my son to a young mothers' group," says one mom, "where I can relate to other young mothers and my son can get to know children his age."[9]

Some support groups also get together for "field trips." Other moms come together for a Girls' Night Out.

To find support groups in your area, call community resources such as pregnancy care centers, your local hospital, or organizations that provide help to mothers, such as the federally funded Women Infants Children Program (WIC) and Teen MOPS.[10]

Mom and Dad

> The first half of our lives is controlled by our parents; the second half of our lives is controlled by our children.
>
> — Anonymous[11]

Another place many young moms turn to for help is from Mom and Dad. While parents can be very helpful, some young moms complain that their parents want to make all the decisions concerning the baby. Other parents don't help enough. One thing to realize is that this is *your* baby. Your responsibility — not theirs.

Life as I See It

I get help from my mum or my fiancé's mum because they have been through the parenting stages.

— Sarah, Sydney, Australia

My husband, my friends, and my father support me. Having people to talk to, cry to, and lean on helps so much. My father has also saved us from being homeless or foodless a couple of times.

— Travis, Michigan

My mom helps me out sometimes, like the other day I was up with my son until 4 a.m. She took him in the morning so I could sleep. She also gives me lots of advice.

— Diana, Washington

If you're getting help from your parents, it's also good to be helpful to them. Don't expect your parents to completely change their lifestyle to fit your needs. Also, don't expect your mom (or dad) to be your only baby-sitter.

Also, consider:

- Your parents aren't as young as you are. Their energy level cannot handle a new baby as well as you can.
- Appreciation goes a long way. Thank your parents for the help they provide. Give small gestures of care back to them, such as a thank-you note, a batch of cookies, or an offer to make dinner.
- Don't expect to get it all for free. If you're living at home, try to contribute something to the household expenses—even a small something. And help with the housework as much as possible. This will show your parents you do care and you are taking your responsibility seriously.
- Work out a contract with your parents. Know what help they are able to provide and what's expected of you in return. Clear communication stops arguments before they start.
- Know that change will come. If you are still at home, do not expect to depend on your parents' good graces forever. Develop both short and long-term goals for your future. Share these goals with your mom and dad and ask for their insight.

• •

Emotional Help

> *Timon:* Gee, he looks blue.
> *Pumbaa:* I'd say brownish gold.
> *Timon:* No, I mean he's depressed.
> *Pumbaa:* Oh.
>
> — From *The Lion King*

Some days everything is great. You get a good grade on a test, your house looks halfway decent, and your child says please.

Then there are those days when life falls apart. The demands on your time, the money challenges, a baby who needs you 24/7. Sometimes you feel like a deflated balloon. You're depleted. Wiped out. When you feel this way, here are some things to consider.

- Let-downs are normal. You are young . . . and you are facing a tremendous amount of responsibility.
- It's okay to cry. Tears have healing properties. Each of us needs a good cry every once in a while.
- Give yourself a break—literally. Forget the dishes for one night. Instead sit outside and enjoy the sunset.
- Seek support, especially if you can't shake your depression. There are many people willing to listen, support you, and give you the help you need.
- Be aware of your feelings towards your baby's father—especially if there are unresolved issues between you and him.

Life as I See It

I find myself frustrated and especially worn out when I get back from school and work. I try to pay lots of attention to my son, but he gets really crabby at that time of day. I know he is probably tired from daycare, but it's so hard. It drives me nuts.

— Diana, Washington

I'm most stressed out when bills are due. Trying to figure out which one I can hold off to pay the others. I never thought groceries would be a financial decision.

— Travis, Michigan

Out of all a young mom's needs, emotional needs are most likely to be ignored. After all, you must eat to live, and you must work to support yourself. But it's much easier to push your emotions deep inside, telling yourself you'll deal with them another day. You may run this way for a while, but you won't run well. And soon you will break down altogether.

"Just as your car runs more smoothly and requires less energy to go faster and farther when the wheels are in perfect alignment," says Brian Tracy, author and speaker, "you perform better when your thoughts, feelings, emotions, goals, and values are in balance."

If this is something you need to work on, don't wait to start. If you find yourself stressed or grumpy:

1. Pause and ask yourself what's causing the problem. Do you need more sleep? Someone to talk to? Time away? Help?

2. Figure out how to have this need met. Even if you have to wait until the weekend to get a baby-sitter, looking forward to a welcome break will lift your spirits.

3. Pray. When I have a bad attitude, I find strength in turning to God. Sometimes the situation changes. But sometimes it's my heart that has the transformation. I can't explain what happens inside, but I've felt a difference time and time again after I pray.

God Can Help

When God measures a woman, He puts the tape around the heart instead of the head.

— Anonymous

Even if you have a great husband, a helpful family, and supportive friends, there will always be times when you need a little more help. People—as great as they are—cannot give you all the help you need. Only God can do that.

And God's not only willing to help, he wants to! The Bible says: "God gives a hand to those down on their luck, gives a fresh start to those ready to quit . . . God's there listening for all who pray, for all who pray and mean it" (Psalm 145:14, 19 MESSAGE).

Personally, I've received help from God when no one else could help me.

- He's given me hope when I've been disappointed.
- He's given me courage when I didn't think I could go on.
- He's given me patience when all I've wanted to do is scream.
- He's even provided for my needs (physical, emotional, financial) when my eyes could see no way.

If you're wondering how you can get this type of help, all you have to do is ask. A fancy term for talking to God is prayer. But God doesn't need anything fancy. He just wants you to talk to him. Why don't you try asking for help from the ultimate Helper? You won't be disappointed!

Life as I See It

I can lift my head as a young mom because I know the closer I get to God, the better the mom he makes me. I don't think I would even be married today if it weren't for God. He has been my strength.

—Laticia, Oklahoma

Your Turn

4U2 Try 1

The Broken Doll

What type of help do you need? Sometimes the best way to learn to receive help is to give it.

One day my young daughter was late coming home from school. I was both annoyed and worried. When she came through the door, I demanded in my upset tone that she explain why she was late.

She said, "Mommy, I was walking home with Julie, and halfway home, Julie dropped her doll, and it broke into lots of little pieces."

"Oh, honey," I replied, "you were late because you helped Julie pick up the pieces of her doll to put them back together."

In her young and innocent voice, my daughter said, "No, Mommy. I didn't know how to fix the doll. I just stayed to help Julie cry."[12]

Think of three things you can do for a special friend today. Maybe she needs physical help, such as child care, a meal, or someone to wash the dishes. Or perhaps a shared moment of laughter, venting, or tears would help the most. Give her a call to find out. If she says she doesn't think she needs help, set up a time to get together — you may discover needs that she doesn't realize she has.

4U2 Try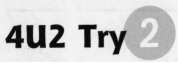

How to Be a Good Parent . . . from a Child's Point of View

1. I feel secure when adults run the household. Be the parent!
2. I feel loved when you care enough to set boundaries. Make and keep rules.
3. I get confused when you are unpredictable. Stay dependable.
4. I'm being me. Accept my immaturity.
5. I'm learning about myself. Teach me to understand my many feelings.
6. I depend on you to teach me correct ways to act. Catch me "being good" and tell me.
7. I can get embarrassed. Correct me in private.
8. I learn when I experience the results of my behavior.
9. Discipline with consequences.
10. I'm full of questions. Tell me answers or I'll get them elsewhere.
11. I need to feel included in the family. Assign household chores.
12. I learn to trust from you. Keep your promises.
13. I need to accept my mistakes. Admit you aren't perfect.
14. I copy your ways of caring for myself. Live a healthy lifestyle.

— Brenda Nixon, Parent Power[13]

4U2 Try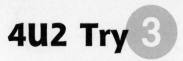

> I pray as if it depended upon God, but I act as if it depended upon me.
>
> — Mother Teresa

If you could completely get rid of one problem today, what would it be? Read this poem and ponder if it *is* possible to let it go.

Let Go and Let God

As children bring their broken toys
with tears for us to mend,
I brought my broken dreams to God
because he is my friend.
But then instead of leaving him
in peace to work alone,
I hung around and tried to help
with ways that were my own.
At last I snatched them back and cried,
"How can you be so slow?"
"My child," he said, "what could I do?
You never did let go."

— Anonymous

Live and Learn

Seeking help enables me to be a capable mother.

7

I need a break
recreation

What is this life if, full of care, we have no time to stand
and stare?

— William H. Davies

Lisa glanced into the rearview mirror as Thomas let out a
squeal.

"Just a minute, pumpkin," she coaxed. "We'll be home in
a few—"

No sooner were the words out of her mouth, than Lisa felt the
car shudder. Then it registered a huge clunk. She'd heard that sound
before. She pulled to the side of the road and jumped out. Thomas
screamed even louder and tugged at the straps on his car seat.

Great, a flat tire. Just what I need.

Lisa popped open her trunk, and pulled out the jack and spare
tire. Thankfully, her dad had insisted she know how to change a flat
before he let her get her driver's license.

Under the hot sun, Lisa quickly changed the flat tire. Thankfully
Thomas had fallen asleep. After putting her tools back in the trunk,
Lisa brushed off her hands, reached for the ignition and then moaned.
A thick line of black grease had streaked her new jeans—the very
jeans she splurged to buy with the last of her paycheck.

What next?

Within a few minutes, she parked the car in front of the apartment she shared with her dad. As soon as the car stopped, Thomas awoke and resumed crying. Lisa carried her son up the two flights of stairs, then made him a peanut butter and jelly sandwich. She turned on *Blue's Clues,* placed him in front of the TV to eat, and hurried back to the car.

As she'd guessed, the ice cream for Thomas's first birthday now dripped from the carton. She hurried upstairs with the groceries, dripping along the way. *Another trip to the store,* Lisa thought as she put things away and sponged up the ice cream drips from the kitchen floor. The credits on *Blue's Clues* were rolling just as she finished. Thomas screamed again, this time pulling at his ear.

Please don't tell me . . . Lisa put her hand against the toddler's forehead. He burned with fever. *Another ear infection.* Lisa sighed. She was supposed to do the wash at the Laundromat today. Her dad needed a clean uniform for work. That was the deal—she did the laundry and housework in exchange for free rent.

Lisa lifted Thomas into her arms and kissed his warm cheek. He rested his head against her shoulder and sucked his fingers, whimpering. There would be no laundry today—only long lines at the clinic with a sick baby.

Back to the car. As she drove by the high school where her friends still attended, Lisa noticed a softball game in progress. The springtime scents of mowed grass and concession-stand hot dogs wafted in the air. Lisa breathed it in. She could imagine the pungent scent of the linseed oil she used to soften her mitt with.

Lisa glanced at the game in progress one last time in her rearview mirror. *I'd give anything to have just one day off. One day of fun—no housework, car problems, or caring for a baby. Just one day.*

24/7

> The watchful mother tarries nigh, though sleep has closed her infant's eyes.
>
> —John Keble, British clergyman and poet

There's a Murphy's Law of Parenting that says:

The later you stay up, the earlier your child will wake up.

For a child to become clean, something else must become dirty.

Toys multiply to fill any space available.

The longer it takes to make a meal, the less your child will like it.[1]

And guess who's doing the staying up, cleaning up, and cooking . . . you! If you're worn out as a mom, you're not alone. All moms feel exhausted and overwhelmed at times. The reasons are clear:

- Lack of sleep
- Too much fast food
- Little exercise
- Frazzled nerves
- Demands that make you try harder, perform better
- No time for fun!

The needs of our children, and our lifestyles, are endless. Where did all our free time go? Not too long ago you may have been a get-out-and-party-girl. Now your idea of fun is squeezing in a few minutes on the phone or vegging in front of the TV. Who has time for recreation?

Life as I See It

Mothering isn't the hard part. It is all my other responsibilities that drag me down—work, school, household chores, and extended family.

—Jessica H.

Free time is spent picking up, zoning out, or catching up on sleep.

— Travis, Michigan

Sometimes I get really stressed about being a single mom. There is never anyone to take over in the middle of the night, or anyone to change half the diapers, or just to take over when you need a nap.

— Jessica, Florida

Moms Need a Break

If you talk to any young mom, she'd agree that taking breaks is important. Yet the "getting away" is the hard part. Sometimes it's challenging due to a packed schedule. Other times it is just too much work—finding a baby-sitter, making plans, and justifying money spent for "fun." It doesn't help matters when you attempt to go out in the evening and your child doesn't want you to go. It's hard to walk away from *those* tears.

Life as I See It

My daughter gets mad when I have to leave her in the mornings. I have to remind myself that kids are more resilient than our guilty conscience would lead us to believe.

— Travis, Michigan

My son initially found it really hard to go to my mom's place. He cried a lot, and it used to tear me up inside. Now he loves going there and rarely cries. They have a much bigger house and more people to interact with.

— Simone, New Zealand

I have a hard time going out because I'm always wondering, How's my daughter? I wonder if she's all right?

— Desiree, Texas

A doctor's appointment must be kept. A trip to town for diapers is a no-brainer. Yet time planned for fun isn't crucial . . . or is it?

- *Having fun makes for fun.* As moms we think that devoting all our time to family responsibilities is part of the job description. Yet how does it make you feel when you follow the same old routine without a break? Listless, tired, bored. A mom who takes time to have fun is a fun mommy to be around.
- *Leisure renews us.* Leisure is another way of saying *time off.* According to the *American Heritage Dictionary* leisure is "freedom from time-consuming duties, responsibilities, or activities." Leisure renews us by giving us relief from stress. It also gives us time to think about what's important to us. "Leisure should be a time to think new thoughts," says author C. Neil Strait.
- *Balance is better.* The ancient Greeks had a saying: *Nothing overmuch.* This phrase speaks of the necessity of balance. Balance is important in work, play, exercise, and even in quietness. It's good to work hard, but be sure to balance work with things that bring you joy.
- *Interests make all areas of life interesting.* "The effect of having other interests beyond those domestic works well," said Amelia Earhart, pioneering pilot from the 1930s. "The more one does and sees and feels, the more one is able to do, and the more genuine may be one's appreciation of fundamental things like home, and love, and understanding companionship."

Life as I See It

I turn on my music whenever I start feeling worn out or am having a hard time with my son. I also drink lots of black tea to keep myself going, and take my son outside as often as possible. (He's much happier outside.) It also refreshes me!

—Simone, New Zealand

Tricia's Blab
Listen up

The dictionary definitions may not have changed since you've had your child, but perhaps your own definitions have.

Time-out *n.* Once thought of as punishment. Now considered as a much-desired, much-deserved break.

Quiet *n.* Once avoided at all cost. (After all, what kind of fun can you have without noise?) Now treasured, sought after, and longed for.

. . . .

Family Time — Fun For Me?

Make a Memory

Make a memory with your children,
Spend some time to show you care;
Toys and trinkets can't replace those
Precious moments that you share.
Money doesn't buy real pleasure,
It doesn't matter where you live;
Children need your own attention,
Something only you can give.
Childhood's days pass all too quickly,
Happy memories all too few;
Plan to do that special something,
Take the time to go or do.
Make a memory with your children,
Take the time in busy days;
Have some fun while they are growing,
Show your love in gentle ways.

—Elaine Hardt, poet[2]

You need a break *from* your child. But if that isn't always possible, take a break *with* your child.

When was the last time you really played with your child? I mean the get-on-the-floor-roll-around-and-act-like-a-puppy type of play? Not too recently? I confess, me neither.

It's hard to take time to play when there are so many other things to do. We feel *guilty*. But guilt shouldn't be a factor. Instead of considering yourself lazy when you take time to play, consider yourself smart. A smart mom knows that the clean laundry won't be remembered as much as the silly-face-game. "It's up to us to seek out the little pieces of life that will become our children's memories," says author Sylvia Harney.[3]

Not only is playing fun, it's important for your child's development. Children learn about the world as they squeeze squeaky toys, crawl under tables, and peek out from behind their blankie. In fact, many developmental experts claim play is the "work" of children.

"A three-year-old child is a being who gets almost as much fun out of a $56 set of swings as he does from finding a small green worm," said journalist Bill Vaughan. Isn't that the truth! How many times has your child ignored the toy while playing with the box it came in? A son of one of my friends loved to play with a bathroom plunger. It was his favorite toy! (Don't worry, she bought a new one just for him.)

But older children shouldn't have all the fun. Babies love songs and fun interaction. You may be surprised how fun and refreshing playtime can be for you too. Here are some fun songs to sing and play. If you can't remember the words ask another mom to help.

- "Peek-a-Boo"
- "Pat-a-Cake"
- "Head-Shoulders-Knees-and-Toes"
- "This Little Piggy"
- "Itsy-Bitsy Spider"

Copy Cat

Not wasting a moment, a child leaps from sleep and skips into a wonder-filled day.

"Ah!" says the wise mother, "An example to follow."[4]

Yet, family time isn't just about playtime. There are quieter, gentler moments that mean just as much.

"As mothers, none of us want to look back in regret that we did not take our children to the playground, kiss them, hold them, and put them to bed," says Heather Hurd, author of *A Book of Hope for Mothers*. "The time we spend with our children when they are young is irreplaceable—for them and for us."[5]

One of my favorite things when my son was a toddler was to lay down with him before nap time. We would sing his favorite songs until his eyelids fluttered and he drifted off to sleep. Sometimes I would stop singing and just listen to his small, squeaky voice. The best part was when he'd forget some words and make up his own—singing with gusto all the same. It was times like this when my son and I learned to enjoy each other's company. And on the occasions when we both drifted to sleep, we just enjoyed being close and listening to each other breathe.

Life as I See It

On the weekends I try to take my son somewhere special, like the beach, getting ice cream, or going for a ride on a train.

— Simone, New Zealand

My idea of fun used to be going out with my friends to the mall, movies, hanging out all night, and driving around town with the top down on the jeep. Now fun is spending time with my baby girl.

— Nina, Texas

. . . .

Laughter

> Laughter is the sun that drives winter from the human face.
> — Victor Hugo, French poet, dramatist, and novelist

What makes you laugh? TV sitcoms? Friends? Your child? Whatever it is, you need more. "People who laugh actually live longer than those who don't laugh," says James Walsh, author of *Laughter and Health*. "Few persons realize that health actually varies according to the amount of laughter."

While comedy is good, one of the most important aspects of laughter is learning to laugh at yourself. Life doesn't have to be as serious as we make it. In fact, life is easier to deal with when we see the humor.

For example, one young mom found humor in a situation that could have upset her.

"One of the funniest things happened on the city bus," she said. "My son and I were out for the day and an older lady began asking about my son. She said, 'His mother must be very proud of him.' She thought I was baby-sitting! I had a good laugh about that later."[6]

Life as I See It

I laugh at silly faces, funny voices. Seeing my son put on a dragon costume and a nurse's headband, saying "Mommy, I'm a dragon nurse!"

— Simone, New Zealand

I love my daughter's funny faces, cute giggles, silly dancing, talking to the cat, and getting applesauce in her hair and mashed potatoes in her nose.

— Travis, Michigan

Laughter is my therapy. It's how I make sense of this crazy life. I laugh at life and keep going!

— Travis, Michigan

Why Laugh?

- *For the exercise.* Author Norman Cousins once said, "Hearty laughter is a good way to jog internally without having to go outdoors." Did you realize a hundred good laughs have been compared to ten minutes of rowing?
- *For the community.* Want to get to know someone better? "Laughter is the shortest distance between two people," says Victor Borge, Danish entertainer and pianist. When you laugh with someone a special, unexplainable bond is formed.
- *As a stress-reliever.* "Laughter is a powerful way to reduce tension and stress, creating a sense of well-being, increasing contentment and alertness, helping us place the problems and difficulties of life in context," says Dr. Patrick Dixon, an English physician and author.
- *For good health.* "The two best physicians of them all are Dr. Laughter and Dr. Sleep," quips writer Gregory Dean Jr.

Exercise!

There are some people who love exercise. For the rest of us, we do it because we know our muscles need to be strengthened, our heart needs to pump, and our pores need to sweat. "But why should I?" you ask? "After all—"

- I power-lift my twenty-pound baby from his crib, morning, nap, and night.
- I do "buns-of-steal" squats, picking up toys off the floor and putting them into the toy box.

- I work my biceps and triceps twenty reps a night, scraping strained peas, carrots, and squash off the kitchen floor.
- I get a cardio workout, running after my fifteen-month-old.

Yes, being a mom is a good workout, but we also need to make time for planned exercise, such as going for a walk or playing tennis with a friend.

"Like it or not—and I don't always like it!—good physical condition (or lack thereof!) does play a crucial part in our climb to sanity,"[7] says Julie Ann Barnhill, author of *She's Gonna Blow.*

The physical benefits are easy to see:

- Stronger heart
- Weight control
- More energy
- Increased strength
- Greater ability to fight illness
- Clearer thoughts

And there are also the spiritual and mental benefits.

"I have a much more positive mood after I've gone for a walk," says one young mom. "It speeds up my metabolism, and I can think more clearly and feel more refreshed."[8]

For myself, when I take time to exercise I start out grumpy, depressed, and overwhelmed, but as I move—the irritations seem to scatter. My problems may not be solved when I finish exercising, but I feel stronger and ready to tackle them.

Life as I See It

My favorite recreation is jogging. Since I started, I have felt so much happier! I feel free from everything. It's twenty minutes when I don't have to worry.

—Amanda, Ontario, Canada

I aim to exercise at least three nights a week. I try not to think of it as a "lose weight" thing, but as a "get more energy" thing. It's a cliché, but it does clear your mind.

— Travis, Michigan

Young Fun

> Live and work but do not forget to play, to have fun in life
> and really enjoy it.
>
> — Eileen Caddy, writer

How would you define fun? I'm sure your definition has changed since becoming a mother. Sometimes it's as if you're pacing the sidelines with your baby while everyone your age tries on silly outfits at the mall, primps for the prom, or rides the rapids on their senior trip. Normal teen stuff seems far away.

But maybe your idea of fun has changed for the better. Many young moms I've talked to say having their babies took them out of destructive lifestyles.

"I was a pretty crazy person before I had my son; getting into trouble was fun for me," said one young mom. "Now fun is spending time with my family, going to the park, and watching my son learn and grow."[9]

There are others who try to mix both worlds—being a teen and a mom. "For fun I hang out with friends, go to dance clubs, bookstores, and take my daughter to the park for walks," said another young mom.[10]

Becoming a mom doesn't mean you have to give up *everything* fun about being young. It doesn't mean you have to wear sweats all day, or go to bed at 9:00 p.m. But it does mean being responsible for the type of fun you choose.

It also may mean making choices that your friends don't understand. There will be times when you'll have to say no to inappropriate fun, like wild parties or all-night street dances.

For me, before I had my son, a good party or driving around in search of hot guys was my idea of fun. Afterward, it had no appeal. I didn't want to take my baby into that atmosphere. But not only that, as I grew up a little, those activities no longer sounded fun.

And boy, am I glad. When my son was a few years old, I ran into some of my old friends. By this time I was attending college and enjoying time with my son and new husband. Yet, they were still doing the same old thing: searching for the perfect weekend party.

"When I first had my daughter—being a breast-feeding young mom—I couldn't just go 'out' with the girls anymore," said one young mom. "The sad part is most of them still don't get it!"[11]

Of course, there are still things you can do with your friends. Here are some ideas:

- After the baby's snuggled in her crib, you can have good friends over to watch a movie and munch on popcorn.
- Do each other's nails like you did when you were kids!
- Cook a gourmet dinner together.
- Go to the beach and play in the sand.
- Take a "road trip" and visit local attractions within an hour's drive.
- Plan a "just because" party, complete with a cake and party hats.
- Get together for a night of board games.
- Start a private reading group, and meet once a month to discuss the books.

Life as I See It

For fun I blow off steam with my girlfriends. We talk, laugh, be silly. If our budget allows, we go out dancing. I write, rent movies, normal stuff. My idea of fun has changed. It's not just "Okay, I need twenty bucks to go out tonight, what am I wearing?" It's more like "Who's babysitting? Okay, she charges ten bucks. How far will I be if I'm needed? If my daughter wakes up at eight a.m., will I be able to deal with five hours' sleep? Are we going someplace safe?"

— Travis, Michigan

Me Time

Recreation isn't always about doing things, going places, and spending time with people. It may mean being alone. Whether or not being alone appeals to you usually depends on how you are wired. Are you an extrovert or an introvert? Don't get scared by these official sounding names, they're easy to understand.

Extrovert. An extrovert gets energized when she's around people. She's most comfortable in social settings and being alone wears her out. She says what she feels (sometimes without thinking), and she isn't afraid to show her emotions. Recreation to an extrovert means doing something with someone else. It's getting out.

Introvert. Spending time alone and gathering her thoughts is what gives the introvert energy. She is more quiet and reserved, and she likes to keep her feelings private. Being around people may make her stressed or overwhelmed. She'd much prefer having a whole day alone to think, read, or do projects.

Of course, most of us are a mix of both. We enjoy being with others, but we need time by ourselves, too. Sometimes your "me" time, can also include "he" or "she" time if you choose to spend it with a husband, boyfriend, or friend. What sounds like fun to you?

Life as I See It

I get refreshed by talking to others. Getting everything that's bottled up out.

— Jessica, Florida

Sometimes I turn up my favorite music really loud and jump and dance around the living room. I also correspond with friends overseas, go to cafes, and go to plays. I daydream about my future—about getting married, about travelling the world, about the different types of work I wanna get into.

— Simone, New Zealand

My "me time" is when my daughter goes to bed. That's when I do housework, take a bath, and read. It's my time to get things done around the house and to pamper myself.

— Jamie, Montana

Feed Your Spirit

Just like our minds and bodies need time to get refreshed, our spirits need replenishment as well. I know my day always goes better when I take time at the beginning to read my Bible, pray, and spend time with God.

In the Bible, Psalms 63:1 talks about an inner thirst for God. David, a king of Israel, wrote, "O God, you are my God, earnestly I seek you; my soul thirsts for you, my body longs for you, in a dry and weary land where there is no water."

If your inner spirit feels discontent—feels like it's missing something—time with God may be exactly what you need. Feeding your spirit doesn't have to be mystical and weird. And you don't have to wait to attend church on Sunday to give it a try. You can:

- Pause and say "thank you" when you see a lovely sunset.
- Pull out your Bible and read a few Scripture verses when your child is taking a nap.

- Write a letter to God, letting him know how you feel.
- Sing an old Sunday school song to your child.
- Talk with a friend, sharing the good things God has done in your life recently. And listen as she does the same.

Life as I See It

There are times where I doubt myself, where I think that nobody cares, where I just don't know if I can keep going anymore—that's when I pray. I find that after I pray I feel like a huge burden has been lifted off my shoulders, and I feel this deep sense of peace.

—Simone, New Zealand

If you're ready for some recreation—whether it involves your mind, body, or spirit, check out the Your Turn activities for fresh ideas!

Your Turn

4U2 Try 1

New Ways for Having Fun

When you make plans with friends, your guy, or your child, do you do the same old things because it's what you've always done? Take a moment to think outside the box. Think about adventure and variety. Then fill in these blanks:

- Next time I got out to eat, one new food I'd like to try is:

  _____

- One fun activity I'd like to attempt is: _____

- Someone who seems fun to hang out with is: _____

Also, now that you're a mom, you should think about "wise fun." Here are some questions to ask yourself before going out:

- Is this a safe and secure environment?
- Do the people I'm with respect me? Are they caring and supportive?
- Is this an environment where sincere, trusting relationships can be built?

Finally, remember the delightful experiences you had as a child and try to recreate them.

- The things that made me laugh were: _____
- The things I liked doing with friends were: _____
- One thing I enjoyed and I want to do with my child is: _____

_____

4U2 Try 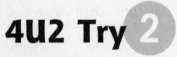 2

Ax the Guilt

Ever feel guilty for having time away? Read this poem.

> Mother-guilt is attached to the umbilical cord, but it stays with you for life.
> You feel guilty about what you do and guilty about what you don't do.
> Guilty when you leave them and guilty when you pick them up.
> Guilty about what they eat, what they don't eat, and even what they might eat.
> The guilt gets you at night, on the train, standing in the school playground, and especially when you've left them when you have a break.
> Then it usually gets attached to your purse and leads you to a toyshop.
> What mothers need is a jury of twelve good and true mothers to stand up and say, "Not guilty, your Honor."[12]

List five things you feel guilty about. Then . . . take time to consider this question: *Should these things make me feel guilty?*

4U2 Try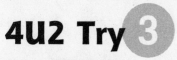

Humor Collection

Need a good laugh now and then? Create your own laughter by starting a "Giggles, Hoots and Chuckles Collection."

- Cut out cartoons from the newspaper and post them on the refrigerator.
- Buy old videos or record TV shows that make you laugh.
- Write down the funny things your child says or does.
- Check out goofy joke books from the library.
- Keep a journal of humorous things that happen to you.
- Pick up "gag" costume pieces such as glasses, noses, and funny hats. Keep them around for days you just want to goof off.

Here are a few jokes to get you started:

- Mother's Day gas station ad: "Free rose for Mother with gas."[13]
- Those who are too concerned about the overpopulation of the earth have no reason to worry. Eventually there will be standing room only. At that point, births will decrease dramatically.[14]
- For several months a little boy had been watching his mother's stomach increase in size. It was becoming harder and harder to sit on her lap. "Mommy, why is your stomach getting so big?" He was told that his little sister was inside her stomach. "Mommy, why is my little sister inside your stomach?" He was told that he used to be in her stomach too. When the boy's father got home, the boy asked his father if he could talk to him in private. They went to the boy's room. "Daddy I need answers to two questions:

First, why does Mommy keep eating little kids? And second, how did I escape?"[15]

4U2 Try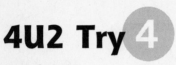

Just for Fun

Want something fun to do with your child? Try this:

- Build a "fort" with pillows and couch cushions. Wad up newspaper to make balls. Then take turns tossing the balls into the fort, with someone inside to catch the balls.
- Build a dollhouse together using boxes. Ask your child to find small objects to use as furniture.
- Read a book aloud while the rest of the family listens and paints with watercolors.
- Let your child help you make play dough by mixing one part water, one part salt, and three parts flour. Then be sculptors.
- Make "ooze dough" by mixing two parts cornstarch and one part water. See what you can do with it. Swirl different colors of food coloring into it.
- Make hand shadows on the wall by darkening the room and shining a light on your hands.
- Play some of your child's favorite music, and move to the music together.[16]

Live and Learn

A happy, relaxed mom makes a happy, relaxed home.

8

what's most important?
perspective

Greatness is to take the common things of life and walk
truly among them.

— Ralph Iron, author

Liz zipped through her apartment on a mission. She thought
she'd have time to wash the dishes left in the sink and maybe
vacuum before Dustin arrived. They'd been dating for two
weeks, and this would be his first time in her apartment. They were
going to watch a movie and have popcorn.

She'd met Dustin at school. He was kind, respectful, and hard-
working. His truck was also immaculate, and she didn't want him
to see her apartment this way.

Kace, Liz's small son, cooed from the swing. He rocked with an
easy rhythm as Liz washed the dishes, then quickly wiped down the
counter. She crammed the large pizza box into the trash, then tack-
led the pile of mail overtaking the counter. Kace began to fuss as Liz
pulled the vacuum from the closet.

"Not now." Liz hurried to plug it in.

The baby's cries escalated. Liz attempted to rock him in one arm
while she vacuumed with the other. It wasn't working. Kace cried
even harder and sucked on his fist.

"Don't tell me you're hungry again."

The room was half-vacuumed, but she had no choice. Liz turned off the machine and settled into the rocker with a loud sigh. Kace stopped crying, latched on, and gazed up at her adoringly. Liz's heart settled as she stroked Kace's cheek. He paused, cooed, then began to nurse again.

"I'm sorry, little guy. Sometimes I get all worked up, and I forget what really matters." She snuggled him close.

"It's you," she whispered. "You're what matters."

Getting Perspective

> You can learn many things from children. How much patience you have, for instance.
> — Franklin P. Jones, writer

Ugh. Sometimes being a parent can be so frustrating. Just as you're finally working on your English essay or you're at a good place in the movie, your child needs your attention. It's as if he has an internal sensor that says, "Start crying, kid. Your mom is *really* busy now."

Of course, when is a good time to be interrupted? Something always fills our time or takes our attention. That's where perspective comes in. Perspective is viewing what happens today in light of the future. It's considering what's really important and contemplating what will matter to us five, ten, or twenty years from now. Then it's planning our time and our goals accordingly.

Life as I See It

My fiancé and I were both excited about my pregnancy until reality set in. Then we were scared that we wouldn't have enough money, enough space in our apartment, and worried that I wouldn't be able to finish school. After we talked to some of our friends, we realized that we had plenty of support and would be able to figure things out.

— Amanda, Ontario, Canada

. . . .

Change of Perspective

When we become mothers we think about things we never considered before—such as being a good role model or scheduling play into our day. We worry about vaccinations, pollution, and too much sexiness on TV. We see the world in a different light, mainly because we've brought a precious child into it.

Life as I See It

Before I was pregnant, all I wanted to do was get out of my mom's house. Now that I have a child, I wish I could just go back and have my mom take care of me—but that's not possible.
— Jessica, Montana

Being a mom has changed the way I think. I worry about things that I never worried about before. We went on vacation, and we had to fly. I have never had any problems with flying, but knowing that my baby was on the plane really upset me.
— Jessica, Florida

If I didn't have my daughter, I wouldn't be going to college or bettering myself. I would be one of those kids you see on the street drunk by noon. When I think of that, I appreciate her that much more.
— Jamie, Montana

Here's another example of perspective:

Once there were two shoe salesmen who went to Africa to open new sales territories. Three days after they arrived, the first salesman faxed a message: "I will be returning on the next plane. I can't sell shoes here. Everyone goes barefoot all the time."

There was no report from the second salesman for about two weeks. Then came a fat, airmail envelope with this message for the home office. "Fifty orders enclosed. Prospects unlimited. Nobody here has shoes."[1]

When you became pregnant, it may have been difficult to consider your pregnancy in a positive light. You may have been like the first shoe salesman who simply focused on the negative and felt like walking away.

Of course you couldn't walk away. You're a mom now. Now you see the world with "mothering" eyes.

You've discovered there is a second way to look at your situation. Like the second salesman, you see the potential. Motherhood has become a time to reconsider your future. A time to clarify your goals. Or maybe it's a time to take a different path.

Making Attitude Adjustments

One of the first things that may have changed when you became pregnant was your attitude. I remember the first few weeks I knew I was expecting. I was sick and miserable. I refused to go to school, refused to leave the house.

Gradually my attitude changed. Instead of feeling sorry for myself, I thought of the good to come out of it. I was going to have a baby—a beautiful baby.

"Our attitude will determine everything in our lives from whom we marry to what we do for a living," says Lucinda Basset, author of *Life without Limits*. "It will determine how we deal with our failures and how and if we achieve our successes; and it will determine our destinies."[2]

Stop and consider your attitude right now. How do you feel about where you are in life? How do you feel about your role as a mother?

Perspective means stopping to consider your various roles. It's weighing the importance of your relationships (as a wife, mom, friend, daughter) in comparison to the tasks you tackle every day. Take a minute and think of all the things you might do in one day.

1. Bathe and dress baby.
2. Fix meals.
3. Attend classes at school.
4. Watch television.
5. Talk on the phone with friends.
6. Visit your mom.
7. Read to your child.
8. Clean the kitchen.
9. Invite a friend over for a meal.
10. Surf on the internet.
11. Go to work.
12. Shop at the mall.
13. Call your grandma.
14. Read your Bible and pray.
15. Watch music videos.
16. Meet friends at the park.
17. Do laundry.
18. Go out drinking with friends.
19. Play with your child on the floor.
20. Spend quiet time talking with your husband or boyfriend.
21. Complete a project at work.
22. Write in your journal.

Now ask yourself these questions.

1. Which tasks help you to contribute to what's most important?
2. Which ones do you wish you had more time for?
3. Which ones would you consider time-wasters?
4. How has your perspective changed after having your child?
5. Are there areas you need to look at with a new perspective?

Life as I See It

It helps to remember my child will only be two once. I don't know God's plans for the future, and I need to make the best of the time I have.

— Katherine, Texas

· ·

Future Thinking

> Alice said, "Would you tell me, please, which way I ought to go from here?"
>
> The Cheshire Cat responded, "That depends a good deal on where you want to get to."
>
> Alice replied, "I don't much care where."
>
> The Cheshire Cat responded, "Then, it does not matter which way you go. Any road will take you there!"
> — From *Alice's Adventures in Wonderland* by Lewis Carol

Where do you want to go from here? Just as the Cheshire Cat reminded Alice, you have to know where you're going if you want to get there.

Giving Up versus Looking Up

In working with young moms, I've seen two paths they usually choose between. Some young moms feel that after having children their lives are out of control — so why bother? They've given up plans for college and instead try to find any job to bring in money. They live where it's convenient, even if the neighborhood isn't very good. They hang out with anyone available, because any friend is better than no friend. They have a new relationship every month. Their perspective is short-range, and their future thinking doesn't go beyond what movie to watch next weekend.

There's a second group. They have a different perspective. Even though it takes more effort, these moms weigh their education options. They seek out appropriate day care and work at jobs with opportunity for promotion. These young moms think of future careers and trust that the time and energy they put into their goals will someday be rewarded. They either commit themselves to a relationship or only date guys that fit their requirements for a lifelong partner.

Which path are you taking?

Of course, just because we take time to plan our future goals doesn't mean we're in control of our futures—no one is. Your baby gets an earache the day of your final. You discover a spit-up stain on your nicest skirt right before a job interview. Your car breaks down. Your company orders layoffs.

Future thinkers take these things in consideration and are willing to rework their goals. Future thinkers trust in God. A God who *is* in control. They pray about their decisions, understanding God sees the bigger picture. The well-known "Serenity Prayer," often attributed to theologian Reinhold Niebuhr, conveys this perspective well:

> God, grant me the serenity to accept what cannot be changed,
> Courage to change what should be changed.
> And the wisdom to know the difference.

Life as I See It

Getting pregnant was definitely a life-changing experience. I have become closer to God and overall a better person.

— Katherine, Texas

When I need some perspective, I turn to my grandma. In a time where woman's liberation is so dominant, I need a little old-fashioned advice. She reminds me of who God made me first: His child, a wife, and a mother.

— Laticia, Oklahoma

Looking at the "bigger picture" of parenting helps me to realize that my current situation will improve. It is just a matter of faith, time, and hard work. My son will get older, make friends, go to school, need me less. I will finish my studies, get a job, and have more time and money to pursue my dreams and goals.

— Simone, New Zealand

The Familiar Way versus the Right Way

If you could change one thing that you find yourself doing over and over again, what would it be? For me it's not paying attention when my children are talking to me. "Uh-huh," I answer automatically, without taking time to turn, make eye contact, and listen.

The following poem talks about one of the biggest challenges that we face when it comes to doing what's familiar. See if you can guess what it is.

Who Am I?

I am your constant companion. I am
your greatest helper or heaviest burden.
I will push you onward or drag you down
to failure. I am completely at your command.
Half the things I do you might just as well
turn over to me and I will be able to do
them quickly and correctly.

I am easily managed—you must merely
be firm with me. Show me exactly how you
want something done and after a few
lessons I will do it automatically. I am the
servant of all great individuals and, alas, of
all failures, as well. Those who are great, I
have made great. Those who are failures,
I have made failures.

I am not a machine, though I work
with all the precision of a machine plus
the intelligence of a human. You may run
me for profit or run me for ruin—it
makes no difference in me.

Take me, train me, be firm with me,
and I will place the world at your feet. Be
easy with me and I will destroy you.

Who am I?

I am Habit.[3]

Did you guess it correctly? Reading this poem opened my eyes too. It made me consider how many things I did just because that was the familiar way of doing them. It also made me consider my habits—the ones that help me and the ones that hurt me.

For example, one good habit I have is waking up early. Although it took planning to develop this habit (setting the alarm clock earlier each day), it's been worth the effort. I enjoy the quiet mornings when everyone else is asleep. It's then that I have time to pray, read my Bible, and contemplate my goals and dreams.

Then there are those habits I'd wish I'd break, like piling items at the bottom of the stairs because I don't want to make the effort to climb the stairs and put them away. This habit not only leads to clutter but can cause someone to trip and fall.

Life as I See It

Parenting is scary. It has to be one of the hardest things to do. Deciding limitations, punishments, rules, expression of love and other emotions, there's so much to consider and decide on. No one's perfect, but any "good parent" tries to do their best.

— Katherine, Texas

Many Things Half-Done versus a Few Done Well

As moms we want to do it all. Keep a perfect house. Be a perfect student. Love our friends and family in abundance. Of course, we can't do all these things perfectly.

The cartoon character Charlie Brown once said, "In the book of life, the answers aren't in the back." That's the truth! The answers of how and where you spend your time and energy are something you have to figure out. Here are some considerations to get you started:

- *Realize that time is limited.* We know this, but do we *really* live by it? In the Bible, King David says, "Teach us to number our days and recognize how few they are; help us to spend them as we should" (Psalm 90:12 LB). This is awesome advice.
- *Realize that people matter most.* I've heard it said that you can tell which things people care about most by looking at their calendars and their checkbook. What do these two things say about you? Are you giving your time and money to things . . . or to people? Things rust, break, and go out of style. Heart connections with people last a lifetime.

Life as I See It

Sometimes it's hard to keep my focus. I have so many things going at once. So many things I need to get done. It can become overwhelming. It can be frustrating and confusing.

— Katherine, Texas

- *Realize it's better to do a few things well.* If you could only do a few things well, what would they be? If you spent ten years working at your fiction-writing skills, you might be able to have a novel published. You'd find the same type of success if you worked ten years as a painter or sculptor. And just think what type of parent you could be if you spent ten years working at being the best one possible!

This is not to say that you should give up housework, focusing only on your child. But when it comes down to having a perfectly clean kitchen or spending a perfectly wonderful day with your toddler, there's only one thing that matters most.

Pearls of Wisdom

If you plant for days—plant flowers.
If you plant for years—plant trees.
If you plant for eternity—plant people.[4]

Priorities Mean Treasuring Every Moment

> Someone once told me that time is a predator that stalks us all our lives. But maybe time is also a companion . . . who goes with us on a journey and reminds us to cherish the moments of our lives—because they will never come again. We are, after all, only mortal.
>   —Captain Jean-Luc Picard, *Star Trek: The Next Generation*

I have to admit there have been many times when I've daydreamed about my children getting older. I try to imagine strolling through my home without tripping over a jumble of toys, or getting lost in a good book without being interrupted by children's shrieks.

Then the day came when I got a taste of what this would be like. My kids were spending the night with their grandparents. My house was quiet. The toys stayed obediently in their toy box, but surprisingly, I didn't like it. When the next morning dawned, I was happy to have them back. I missed the smiles and laughter. Dare I say it—I even missed the noise!

Sometimes when you're in the middle of a "parenting moment" it's hard to appreciate being a mom. My grandma is good at reminding me of how precious these moments are. "These are the best years of your life," she often tells me when I call. "Enjoy every moment."

Another thing that helps me to enjoy my children is remembering how I almost lost my oldest son. I had just turned eighteen and was still trying to get used to the parenting thing, when Cory became sick. He cried constantly and wouldn't eat. He had a slight fever, but nothing too bad. I took him to the health clinic.

"It's just colic," the doctor said.

So I wrapped up my baby and took him home. But still, something was not right. His fever spiked to 103 degrees and the crying wouldn't stop. The next day I took him to the emergency room where the doctor diagnosed spinal meningitis. There was a chance that he wasn't going to make it.

As they worked on my baby, putting IVs in him, trying to get fluid and antibiotics into his system, I prayed like I never had before. A year earlier my pregnancy had been a crisis, but now I couldn't imagine life without my son.

The prayers, and the expert care of the doctors and nurses, worked. After a week my son was out of the hospital. He was his happy self again. I was grateful. I also understood even better that life is precious.

Life as I See It

As a young mom it's hard sometimes. I see other teens and the life they live. They are so carefree and irresponsible. For a millisecond I think, "That could have been me." Then God gives me a reality check. Like having my four-year-old say, "You are the best mommy ever." Or my baby will touch my face and smile. Those things bring me back to what's important.

— Laticia, Oklahoma

What Are Your Priorities?

From the beginning, I knew that spending all the time I could with my son was important. But being young, I also knew that graduating from high school and attending college classes would benefit us both. I made it a priority to work on my education. It meant finding good child care and spending late nights doing homework after my son went to bed. But the benefits of my school years can't be denied. Education—both formal and informal—has transformed me into a mother my son can be proud of. And a woman I can be proud of.

Once I got married, my husband became a major priority too. From early in our marriage I have taken time to show him he's important. I chat with him while he gets ready for work. I iron his shirts to save him time. I even watch sci-fi movies with him occasionally. We talk and laugh together and consider each other best friends.

My kids are also a top priority. At a time in my life when outside activities such as book clubs or coffee time with friends interest me, I instead choose to spend time at home with my kids. When I'm able, I catch up with friends after my kids go to bed for the night.

Of course, I don't always know what's best at all times. I make choices, then I change my mind. I make commitments to stay close to home, and then I seek out friends because I feel lonely. One week I'll be on a "health food" kick, and I'll break out my low-fat cookbook and marvel my family with culinary creations. The next week, I'll get involved in a new project, and we're scarfing chicken fingers and mac 'n cheese.

Yet even when I change my mind and my daily priorities, I still keep things in perspective: God, husband, family, home, friends, work. I still try to consider how today's decisions affect my goals for the future.

Time Waits for No One

To realize the value of one year: ask a student who has failed a final exam.

To realize the value of one month: ask a mother who has given a birth to a premature baby.

To realize the value of one week: ask an editor of a weekly newspaper.

To realize the value of one hour: ask the lovers who are waiting to meet.

To realize the value of one minute: ask the person who has missed the train, bus, or plane.

To realize the value of one second: ask a person who has won a silver medal in the Olympics.

Time waits for no one. Treasure every moment you have!

—Author Unknown

Balance

> In the end . . .
> *all* of life
> *all* of mothering
> is *all* about balance.

Having balance means:

- Loving your child, yet taking care to discipline.
- Not focusing solely on your child, yet giving her the attention she needs.
- Providing friendship, and accepting friendship in return.
- Looking for a heart-companion, yet becoming the person someone else can give his heart to.

Balance is:

- Planning for the future, yet trusting in a God who knows what's best.
- Working toward your education, but not getting too wrapped up in success.
- Telling someone what's on your heart, and taking time to listen.
- Being a mom your child needs, yet stealing moments to contemplate your unique dreams.

If someone figured out how to balance all of life perfectly, her book would hit the *New York Times* best-seller list, and she'd be invited to every talk show from *Oprah* to *20/20*. Yet seeking balance doesn't mean finding one place—one perfect schedule—and sticking to it.

"Up-and-down rhythm can actually keep . . . life moving in a positive direction. Our lives are meant to be dynamic, not static," says Joanna Weaver, author of *Having a Mary Heart in a Martha World*. "Like a clock pendulum or the pump of an oil well, the rhythm actually generates energy for our lives. The truth is, we thrive on a life that is rhythmically balanced, not standing still."[5]

Yes, no. Work, play. Move forward, rest a while. Keeping life in perspective, keeping God and relationships in perspective will bring rhythmic balance to your life and your mothering. Check out Your Turn activities which will help you do just that!

Your Turn

4U2 Try 1

What Pop Culture Tells Us

That size 12 is big.

That we must dress right, or end up in a "don't" column.

That we must constantly seek perfection.

The same information every month with different titles.

How to cook, eat, dress, behave, and think.[6]

Too many times we get our perspective from magazines that display airbrushed models on their covers. Or from TV sitcoms where the scriptwriter, set director, and hair and makeup artist all work together to portray "life."

Personally, I get in trouble when:

- The latest catalogue makes me feel my clothes are "out of fashion."
- The slim models make me feel frumpy and fat.
- The latest issue of *Better Homes and Gardens* makes my own place seem dingy and bland.
- Health magazines make me feel like a failure for not exercising often enough.

What about you?

- How do the models in the magazines you read affect your perspective about yourself?
- How do the articles in parenting magazines make you feel about your parenting abilities?
- How do romantic movies make you feel about being a wife or girlfriend? Or worse yet, how do they make you feel if you're single?

- How do songs on the radio make you feel about life? Excited? Hopeless? Do they make you think of life as a gift?

Next time you're reading a magazine, watching a movie, or listening to music, consider how you feel. Nix any media outlets that make you have a negative perspective on your life, your parenting, and yourself. Replace it with media that will encourage and inspire you. Then weigh how your perspective changes for the better.

4U2 Try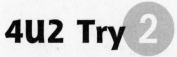

It's What You Do Afterward That Counts

Here's some wise insight from *Buffy the Vampire Slayer:* "There's moments in your life that make you . . . that set the course for who you're gonna be. Sometimes they're little subtle moments. Sometimes they're not. Bottom line is even when you see them coming, you're not ready for the big moments. Nobody asks for their life to change. Not really, but it does. So what are we helpless? Puppets? No, the big moments are gonna come. You can't help that. It's what you do afterward that counts. That's when you find out who you are."

You may not have seen your pregnancy coming, or the changes that mothering would bring to your life. But "what you did afterward" is what counts. Take a moment and consider the things you did right:

- What did you do afterward concerning work or school?
- What did you do afterward concerning your friendships and other relationships?
- What did you do to help you become a good parent?
- What planning have you done toward a better future?

Now ask yourself what you can do from this moment on to improve each of these areas.

4U2 Try 3

An Example of True Love

An old man got on a bus one February 14 carrying a dozen red roses. He sat beside a young man. The young man looked at the roses and said, "Somebody's going to get a beautiful Valentine's Day gift."

"Yes," said the old man.

A few minutes went by and the old man noticed that his young companion was staring at the roses. "Do you have a girlfriend?" the old man asked.

"I do," said the young man. "I'm going to see her now. I'm taking her this." He held up a Valentine's Day card.

They rode along in silence for another ten minutes, and the old man rose to get off the bus. As he stepped out into the aisle, he suddenly placed the roses on the young man's lap and said, "I think my wife would want you to have these. I'll let her know that I gave them to you."

He left the bus quickly, and as the bus pulled away, the young man turned to see the old man enter the gates of a cemetery.

— Author Unknown[7]

None of us like the thought of losing the ones we love. How does this story put life and love into perspective for you?

If you could do anything for the person you love right now, what would it be?

What's stopping you?

4U2 Try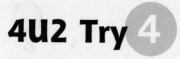

Take a couple of minutes and consider your habits. Jot down your answers to these questions:

- What habits have helped you in life?
- What habits do you wish you could get rid of?
- What got you started on these bad habits?
- How did you train yourself for the good habits?
- How can you turn the bad habits into good ones?
- How do habits affect your parenting?
- Do you treat your child the way your parents treated you out of habit?
- How would you really like to treat them?

This, my friend, is perspective.

Live and Learn

Perspective helps me to focus on what matters most.

9

what am I here for?
hope

Some things you see with your eyes; others you see with
your heart.

— From the movie *The Land before Time*

The alarm clock screeched, and Alison stretched her arm toward the nightstand. "Tell me it's not morning already," she moaned.

Wayward curls stuck to her cheek. Her mouth felt sticky and dry. And her head—a heavy ache radiated from each temple, making it difficult to open her eyes. It had only been three hours since she'd fallen into bed after working late. Her body screamed for more sleep.

Her stomach growled, but she knew that she'd eaten the last of the cereal yesterday. Maybe she'd have time to scramble an egg—if Josie didn't wake up too soon.

As if on cue, the baby's cry echoed from the other room.

"Maaa, maaa—" the small voice wailed.

Alison stood, kicked through a pile of laundry, and stalked toward the kitchen. A job application, a college schedule, and various overdue bills were spread across the counter like playing cards. Alison glanced through blurry eyes at the note from the welfare department. She had sought information about child support from Josie's father, but apparently Roger couldn't be found. The department said they'd keep looking, but it didn't matter. Even if they did find him he wouldn't have any money. *Creep.*

"Maa, maa—" the voice called again.

"Just a minute!" Alison could hear Josie's tiny fist knocking on the wall next to her crib. "I'll be right there!"

Alison opened the fridge and pulled out a jar of applesauce. She grabbed the last packet of instant oatmeal from the cupboard—Josie's breakfast.

Alison placed them on the counter and headed toward her daughter's bedroom. Rounding the corner, her pinky toe smashed against the wall. "Ouch!" She grabbed her toe. "Stupid wall!"

Josie's crying began again, and Alison was sure her head would explode. More than anything she wanted to go back to bed and sleep for a week.

Alison pulled Josie from her crib. The baby's diaper was soaked—and Alison had forgotten to buy more diapers. *What am I going to do now?* Alison knew she didn't have time to stop by the store before class, and she couldn't take Josie to day care soaking wet.

Alison slumped to the floor, and Josie crawled toward a pile of stuffed animals. Alison watched her beautiful daughter play, her throat thickening with emotion.

What am I going to do? I can't handle this. How can I give this child what she deserves? She wiped warm tears from her cheeks. *Is there any hope?*

. . . .

Hopeless Situations

Young moms need hope ...

When sleep is a distant memory.

When your sweet little baby transforms into a monster-toddler.

When you have ten dollars for the rest of the week.

When the only "men" who pay attention to you are your son ...
and your little brother.

When your best friend no longer calls.

When your schoolwork doesn't get done because you have to
work late.

When life isn't what you signed up for.

When your "fat" clothes have replaced your "skinny" ones.

When you long for someone who understands.

When life seems hopeless ...

—Tricia Goyer

Have you ever felt hopeless? I can only guess the things that rob your optimism: guy problems, money issues, overwhelming responsibilities.

But those are only outside struggles. There are inside ones too. Sometimes you feel loneliness, heartache, anger, and despair. Other times there's simply an unsettled feeling deep in your gut. A feeling that tells you something isn't right. A feeling that prods you to question if there's more to life than *this*.

That's where hope comes in.

A glimmer of hope is like lighting a match in a darkened room. It may begin as a small flame, but mixed with the right fuel it has the potential to spread—filling the chamber with both warmth and light.

Life as I See It

I feel like I'm important as a mother. I'm showing people that a young mother is totally capable of raising a baby and finishing high school. I've also faced other challenges. I was diagnosed with anaplastic large-cell lymphoma when my daughter was three months old. I had to drop out of school my second semester and undergo six rounds of chemo while still raising a baby. I have now finished high school and will graduate with my class in May. I feel as though I have shown those around me that you can overcome challenges and make it.

— Desiree, Texas

Happily Ever After

> *Prince Henry:* Will you meet me tomorrow?
> *Danielle:* I shall try.
> *Prince Henry:* Then I shall wait all day.
> — From the movie *Ever After*

I love fairy tales. In fact, *Ever After,* a newer Cinderella story starring Drew Barrymore, is one of my favorite movies. It's a story about a common girl who becomes a princess. The prince not only finds Danielle and carries her away from a despairing lifestyle—he *adores* her.

The Cinderella story has been retold in different ways through the years. In one movie, the woman is a prostitute and the hero is a wealthy businessman. In another, she is a maid and he is a political candidate. In another, she is the homely daughter of Greek parents and he is a dashing American.

Of course, before the "falling in love" part can happen, there's usually some type of transformation that happens within the main character. In Cinderella's case, her darling fairy godmother sweeps in and transforms her ashes into beauty. In *My Big Fat Greek Wedding,* Toula got a makeover and ditched the nerdy glasses. Then she squared her shoulders, realized her worth, and made up her mind to be the person Ian saw her to be.

How many of us wish we could be written into a fairy tale?

"Once upon a time . . ."

"A long-ago time, in a faraway land . . ."

"They lived happily ever after."

To Love and Be Loved

> Sometimes I feel there's a hole inside of me. An emptiness that at times seems to burn . . . I have this dream of being whole. Not going to bed each night wanting. But still sometimes, when the wind is warm or the crickets sing, I dream of a love that even time will lie down and be still for.
>
> — From the movie *Practical Magic*

I've always wanted to love and be loved. It was my dream for every relationship I'd ever been in. From first glance, I wanted to be swept away and adored. I wanted what happened *a long-time ago, in a faraway land* to happen to me. Today. Right where I was. And it did . . .

My Cinderella Story

When I first met Rob (not his real name), I thought he was something special. He was a football player, an honor student, and very handsome too. The best part was, he liked me. I was head-over-heels excited. I thought I was in love.

"Dating" in my small town consisted of being together at dances, at sporting events, and in cars hidden away on dark country roads.

Our relationship became physical even before we had a chance to get to know each other's heart. Then there were the attractions—mine to other guys and his to other girls—that caused all types of problems.

We dated from my sophomore year to my senior year—with more turbulence than a jet plane in a windstorm. When I found out I was pregnant, Rob was already out of the picture.

My parents were upset, but they were committed to helping me stick it out. I'd already had an abortion the previous year—due to Rob's insistence and my own fear—and I wasn't going to make that mistake again. Though he wanted me to have a second abortion, I couldn't do it. I already hated myself for the first one. I lived with the horror of the abortion decision every day and had nightmares about it every night.

You may remember that feeling of attending class, knowing—in secret—that you have a baby growing inside you. I felt hot and tense and unable to focus. Soon, the word got out and rumors spread. Glances were cast my way as I walked down the halls. Whispers behind my back. My friends were awkward around me. Rob began dating someone else. I wanted to move away and never return. The next best thing was for me to drop out of regular school, which I did.

I was sick, tired, and getting bigger by the day. I enrolled in a school for "needy" teens and fit right in.

This all happened during my senior year, and while everyone was attending Homecoming and Prom, I was staying up late watching old movies and sleeping until noon. What had become of my life?

I clearly remember waking up one day and flipping on my favorite soap opera, *The Young and the Restless*. What an appropriate title to what I was feeling.

I rolled to my side, wrapped my arms around my expanding stomach, and considered what a mess I'd made of my life. What happened to my dreams, plans, and goals for a good future?

Then I remembered something. Like a ray from a lighthouse breaking through a foggy coastline, I thought of the stories I'd heard as a child while attending Sunday school. Stories of God. God who loved *me,* not my performance. God who accepted me as I was, without my need to make myself look good.

So at that moment, I prayed. It wasn't elegant but it was from the heart. "Oh God, I've really screwed things up this time. If you can make things better, please try."

And then that beam of light not only touched my memory, but also my heart. And in an unexplainable way, I felt different inside. Something birthed inside me. That something was hope.

> Hope is the thing with feathers
> That perches in the soul,
> And sings the tune without the words
> And never stops at all.
>
> —Emily Dickinson[1]

And at that moment, my soul sang.

I couldn't count on people, but God proved I could count on him. I was unmarried, pregnant, angry, and lonely. God was okay with that. I didn't know where to go or what to do next. But the peace of God told me things would work out. I needed love, and he loved me. He wanted to prove I was someone special in his eyes—even when I felt far from special in my own.

Hope made its home in my heart that day. My life wasn't suddenly "fixed." I still didn't know what to do with the mess I was in. I didn't have all the answers. But hope told me it would be okay. It was a miracle, and I was full of wonder.

Life as I See It

When I place my hope in God, I am more positive, less stressed. I feel free.

—Katherine, Texas

My hope lies in God alone. He has shown me how he can take a steel heart and slowly melt it down. Without God I would probably be out living a single lifestyle—without a husband or God. I would be destroying myself and my kids.

— Laticia, Oklahoma

Here's another story of hope from another young mom.

"My story is kind of different from others. I was passed back and forth from my mom to my grandparents for most of my young life. My mom loved being my friend. It was the mom part she had a problem with. I always felt like I had to take care of her, telling her what was right and wrong.

"When I was thirteen, I decided it was time for me to have a baby of my own. I was very mature for my age, and I almost envied other young moms. I thought to myself, 'They are so cool. If only that was me.'

"So when I was one month away from my fourteenth birthday, I met a guy and decided I would stop my birth control. (Yes, I had birth control at thirteen). Well, it worked, but I had a miscarriage and was devastated. Still, my boyfriend and I stayed together and got married. Three weeks after the honeymoon, I found out I was pregnant again. I was so happy.

"Then came the fear. What if I can't finish school, or what if I can't take care of the baby? I vowed to finish high school and not let my pregnancy change anything.

"All this time I had wanted to be pregnant, but when it happened I started to realize things don't always happen the way we imagine. I had always thought I was grown up, but I was in for an awakening. I had to become a twenty-five-year-old woman overnight. It took some time—and the Lord—to help me mature.

"When I was pregnant, I would be in Wal-Mart and the older women would look and shake their heads. The only way I was able to get through the looks and whispers was my confidence in Christ.

I can lift my head because the closer I came to him the better I became. I don't think I would even be married today if it wasn't for Christ. He has been my strength.

"People always seem to have pity on me and feel sorry for me. But that is only at first. After they talk to me for a while, they see I am not some little girl who doesn't know what she's doing. God gives all of us a purpose and for three years I was looking for mine. God made me a mom. I have found my importance through God. He's given me hope."[2]

Hope Is a Person

Hope is a person, and his name is Jesus Christ. I don't know what that name means to you. Perhaps you've heard it used as a curse word. Perhaps you connect it with people who've told you they were Christians but hurt you deeply. Thankfully, Jesus is big enough to stand on his own two feet. He was a living, breathing person who came to earth with a mission. I'll try to explain it simply.

Jesus was present at the creation of the world. The most prized of all his creation was humankind. God gave man and woman a choice to obey or disobey. They chose the latter, and sin entered into the world. This was no surprise to Jesus. From the beginning, he knew what he would be asked to do.

Thousands of years passed from the time God created the earth until Jesus walked on it, but God was not silent.

He spoke to men and women about freedom from their sins. He spoke in words and through the examples of people's lives. Prophets foretold God coming to earth as man. Believers in God pictured a powerful ruler who would conquer their enemies. Instead, Jesus was far from powerful, if judged in earthly terms. He was not a military ruler. He did not live in a king's castle. In fact, Jesus was born to an unmarried, teen mother.

He was a simple man, a carpenter, who liked to hang out with friends. He liked to talk to people about God in a way they understood. He talked to them through stories.

Jesus hung out with people the religious considered "dirty." He had dinner with prostitutes. His best buddies were uneducated fishermen. He happily spent time with the young moms of the day.

From the time of creation until the days of Jesus' life, God showed his followers a way for men and women to "pay" for their sins. The only way was to sacrifice an innocent lamb. The lamb's death paid for people's sins—sins that were worthy of death.

When Jesus came to earth, he was prepared to pay the price once and for all. Jesus became the sacrificial lamb, and this too was planned from the beginning. By Jesus' death, he conquered sin. And when he rose from the dead three days later, he conquered death.

We too can conquer death when we have faith in what the Bible says. When we have faith that Jesus is the way to God.

John 3:16 says, "This is how much God loved the world: He gave his Son, his one and only Son. And this is why: so that no one need be destroyed; by believing in him, anyone can have a whole and lasting life" (MESSAGE).

All you have to do is believe. And tell him you believe. And your life will change. Like my life, and like the lives of so many more. It just takes one prayer.

Something like this:

Dear Lord Jesus, I believe that you are the prince I have always dreamed of, and you love me completely. I also believe that I was created with an inner desire that only you can fill—with yourself. I need your help. I need the eternal life only you can give. I want to trust you as my Savior. Please accept my prayer. I welcome you into my life. I'm ready to start a relationship with you that will last for my lifetime and beyond. Amen.

If you prayed that prayer as you read it, you can be sure that your life will never be the same! You have reason to hope, not just for good things in this life, but for an eternity with God. You can also be sure that Jesus will assist you in meeting your needs, as you walk through life with him.

. . . .

What a Relationship with Jesus Is All About

It may be hard for you to understand what it means to have a relationship with someone you can't see or touch. When you start any relationship, one of the first things you do is spend time together.

Spending time with Jesus includes reading the Bible, communicating with him in prayer, and watching in eager anticipation what he's doing in your life. It's not easy at first. But remember it's the *beginning* of your relationship. The beginning of something new. The more you interact with Jesus, the more you'll want to:

Read the Bible. The Bible is made up of two sections, the Old Testament and the New Testament. The Old Testament begins with creation and follows the story of God's interaction with people up until four hundred years before Jesus walked on earth.

The New Testament begins with the story of Jesus in the first four books: Matthew, Mark, Luke, and John. It continues by telling about the first Christians and their struggles and triumphs in following Jesus. The New Testament ends with prophecies about the end of our earth as we know it.

The Bible is made up of many types of literature. There is poetry, such as in the book of Psalms; prophecy, such as in the book of Isaiah; and eyewitness reports, such as in the book of John. There also are letters, such as the book of Romans.

There are all styles of Bibles for you too choose from. There are study Bibles that have additional information about the text. There are teen Bibles that have added sections on things that concern young people. There are even Bibles put together especially for moms. These Bibles highlight verses that are useful in parenting. They also have supplemental stories and quotes to encourage you in your mothering. There are also various translations, such as *The Message,* which are written in today's language and are easier to understand.

When you begin to study the Bible, the best place to start is the New Testament—especially the first four books, which describe Jesus' life on earth. Start by simply reading it. Get a feel for the words and the flow. Follow what Jesus did and said. Some stories may seem exciting or amazing. Others may be sad or confusing. Some may even seem strange. But keep reading. It's his way to show us who he is. What a gift!

Pray. Prayer is simply talking with God. You don't have to know any "correct" words or memorize long passages. You can simply tell God how you feel, praise him for what he's doing, and ask him to help you. You can also ask forgiveness when you blow it. Also, no matter what you've seen on TV, you don't have to get on your knees to pray. You can if you want to, but God hears you just the same when you're in bed or jogging through your neighborhood.

Spend time with other Christians. The Bible instructs us to spend time with other people who follow Jesus. They help to encourage us and support us. More experienced Christians are also able to answer our questions by showing us truths in the Bible.

The best place to meet Christians is at church. We don't have to be on this journey by ourselves. Pray and ask God to lead you to a Bible-believing church that will inspire and encourage you. Also know that God's church is more than just a place to visit on Sundays. The church is also the people who join together to share God's love with the world.

Notice when God is at work in your life. One of the best ways to know God is to see what he is doing in your life. Keep a journal of the blessings. (See the Your Turn section.) God takes care of you in many ways. He loves to love you. You just need to have an open heart to see what he's up to.

Hope for All Your Situations

As we look back at the needs discussed in this book, you can see how hope was the final piece.

Do I Matter? (Importance) You do matter, you know. The first chapter discussed many reasons why. We discussed why being a good mom is important, especially for the impact you have on your child. But when it comes to your relationship with God, what matters most is how *God* sees you. You are significant, not because of what you do, but because of who you are. Once you realize your worth to God, you are free to be the mom he designed you to be.

Who Am I? (Identity) You are God's special creation. He designed you exactly how he wanted you, and he loves you just as you are. When you see yourself as God sees you, you don't have to worry about an identity crisis. You are his child. His creation. Trust, rest, and rejoice in the person he made you to be.

Where Am I Going? (Growth) If you could see the potential God has planted inside you, there'd be no holding you back! When you take time to explore your dreams and dare to grow by trusting God to help you, you become more of the person he designed you to be. You also become a gift to those around you, including your child.

Do You Love Me? (Intimacy) When discussing intimacy, we talked about connecting with someone who touches your heart—through communication, time spent together, and love shared. When it comes to perfect love and perfect intimacy, there is only one person who can meet your every need. Only God's love is perfect. Only he can satisfy your deepest heart-longings. God in Jesus Christ came to earth to show us what this love was all about. When you decide to embark on a relationship with Jesus you will discover that his intimacy reaches a place no human can touch.

How Do I Do This Mom Thing? (Instruction) The Bible is the ultimate source of instruction. Jesus says in John 14:6, "I am the way and the truth and the life. No one comes to the Father except through me." When we follow Jesus' instructions we will find the right paths for our future. We will discover truth. And we discover the joy only God can give.

Can You Help? (Help) Sometimes we want God to whisk us out of difficult situations like a rescue helicopter. But honestly, most of the time he lets us struggle through the difficulties. Why? He knows our problems help us to grow. It's how we learn to trust him more. And he loves us enough to want us to depend on him—to seek him out for help.

If we ask for his help, God never makes us struggle alone. His help may be bringing another person into our life. It may be giving us the courage to deal with our bad habits or to get out of a destructive relationship. His help may be providing the strength to attend school, to work, and take care of a baby. Jesus is available 24/7. Just ask.

I Need a Break (Recreation) When God created the world, he worked for six days, then rested on the seventh. He didn't need to take that long. He didn't need a day off. He did it as an example for us. God created within us the need to balance our work with rest. This includes a physical breather—actually setting aside a day for recreation. We don't need to feel guilty for the way we were made. Taking time for recreation is just as important as taking time to meet our other needs!

What's Most Important? (Perspective) Perspective means focusing on what will last—especially our family and relationships. As we focus on God, he shows us what's important. He will point out the things that will last forever. They are the things we will never regret giving our time, energy, and love to.

Your Turn

4U2 Try 1

The Dance

Are you ready for the embrace of a lifetime?

We have a choice every day, you and I.

And it's a choice we make every day, throughout the day.

The choice is:

> We can dance.
> Or we can sit it out.

If we dance, we may step on his toes. And he may step on ours. We may stumble and bump into other people. We may fall on our faces and make fools of ourselves. People may talk, they may avoid us, they may even ridicule us.

If you fear those things, you may want to sit this one out.

If you do, you won't have to worry. You'll be safe in your seat along the wall.

You'll also miss the dance.

More importantly, you'll miss the romance.

At some time or another, I have chosen to sit it out. Fear was a big reason. Fear of the attention it would bring—and perhaps the criticism. Fear of embarrassment and possible estrangement. Fear of not being in control of my life, my career, my future. Fear of being led to places that would be uncomfortable, even painful.

There are two things I have learned from the divine embrace.

Perfect love really does cast out fear.

And I would rather dance poorly with Jesus than sit perfectly with anyone else.

— Ken Gire, *The Divine Embrace*[3]

4U2 Try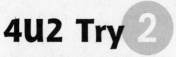

Twelve Reasons to Pray

1. It encourages others.
2. It reminds you of spiritual values.
3. It gives you hope.
4. It helps you feel better.
5. It allows you to let go of situations.
6. It provides comfort.
7. It relaxes you and reduces anxiety.
8. It builds faith.
9. It deepens character.
10. It broadens your perspective.
11. It brings you closer to God.
12. It works.[4]

4U2 Try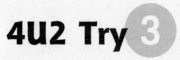

When it comes to praying, there's no formula. It just comes down to talking to God.

Another thing that's good to know is that there are different types of prayers. So if you're ever at loss for words, an easy thing to remember is A.C.T.S.

- **A**doration. This means to worship God and show your love for him. It can go something like this, "God, you are wonderful! You are full of love and goodness!"

- **C**onfession. This is the time that you confess the wrong you have done. They can be big or small. And with your confession, know that God will forgive. Here's an example, "God, forgive me for failing to be loving and patient with others as you have asked me to be."
- **T**hanksgiving. This one is easy. Just thank God for all that he's given you! "God, thank you for my child, my family, my health, and so many other things that I often take for granted."
- **S**upplication. This is a big word that means, "Praying for your needs." Do you need help with school or work? Do you need to find a better job? Or do you need help with potty-training your child? Ask!

4U2 Try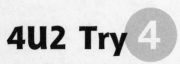

Tips for Reading Your Bible

Just like food nourishes your body, God's Word can feed your soul! Here's how:

Preparation. Before you start, find a quiet place to read where you won't be distracted. Also, pray and ask God to speak to you through his words.

Start with small bites. Don't feel like you have to sit down and read the entire Bible cover to cover. Take in small bites, such as fifteen minutes a day. (In fact, if you consistently read for fifteen minutes a day you will read the whole Bible in one year!)

Digest it. There is a difference between just reading your Bible and really taking it in. To digest God's messages:

1. Read slowly.

2. Pause and think about any passages that stir your imagination.

3. Try to imagine the stories or images in your mind.

4. Write down any questions you may have. Also, write down any meaningful messages that you read.

5. Use study tools found in your Bible to answer your questions. This may include footnotes on the bottom of the page or indexes in the back of the book. Or you can also pick up a good Bible dictionary and other helps in a Bible bookstore or online. If you need more help, ask your mentor or a trusted, godly friend.

Put God's Word to work. Just as food energizes your body, let God's Word energize your life. Memorize short passages by reading them over and over again. Then stop and consider how the passages apply to your everyday circumstances. You may be surprised by how much you'll be able to apply God's concepts to your life!

Share it. Sharing a meal is always more fun when someone else joins you. Find a partner to read God's Word with you. Or perhaps join a Bible study group. Also, write your favorite passages on index cards and pass them out to others who may need encouragement.

4U2 Try 5

God's Delays Are Not Denials

What do you hope for? Are you getting discouraged because your prayers aren't getting answered the way you want as quickly as you'd like? If so, consider the following story.

Never think that God's delays are God's denials. A lone shipwreck survivor on an uninhabited island managed to build a rude hut in which he placed all that he had saved from his sinking ship. He prayed to God for deliverance, and anxiously watched the horizon each day to hail a passing ship. One day he was horrified to find his hut in flames. All that he had was gone. To the man's limited vision, it was the worst that could happen, and he cursed God. Yet the very next day a ship arrived. "We saw your smoke signal!" the captain told him.[5]

This story just goes to show that in your own life there may be times when it seems all is lost, but it is then that you can trust that God has a plan. It's a matter of living by faith, not sight.

4U2 Try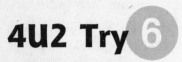

A Blessing Journal

"Each day comes bearing its gifts. Untie the ribbons," says writer Ann Ruth Schabacker. Now, you can count your blessings *and* record them. Start a Blessing Journal.

- *Begin.* Start with a blank book or a spiral-bound notebook.
- *Recollect.* Think over the special gifts given to you throughout the day. They can be anything from a baby's smile to extra hours on your paycheck.
- *Record.* Write down a set number of blessings, or gifts, given to you that day. The end of the day is a good time to do this as you think over the past twenty-four hours. Choose one, three, or five to write down.
- *Focus on the heart.* Don't worry about your handwriting, or if you have a stain from your coffee cup, or even if toddler fingers leave smudge marks. The purpose isn't the words on the page, but the thankfulness in your heart.

- *Be thankful.* As you write each one of your blessings, realize how important each one is. Also, be sure to thank God for loving you so much.
- *Transform.* Over time you'll notice that recording your blessings changes your attitude from one of despair to one of gratitude.
- *Share.* Give the joy of a Blessing Journal to your friends or family. You can keep it simple, or customize it with a picture of you and your baby. You can even sign the front with a special note.

Live and Learn

Hope is a person who loves me completely!

acknowledgments

This book wouldn't be possible without the love and support from my awesome husband, John, and my three wonderful kids: Cory, Leslie, and Nathan. Thank you for encouraging words, back rubs after long days at the computer, and help around the house.

Thanks to those who loved and supported me when I was a teen mother. My mom and grandparents: Linda Martin, and Fred and Dolores Coulter. My father- and mother-in-love: John and Darlyne Goyer. My dad and brother: Ron and Ronnie Waddell.

Thanks to my heart-friends, who offer tons of support: Cindy Martinusen, Twyla Klundt, and Tara Norick.

Thanks to the mentors and *all the teen moms* at Hope Pregnancy Center in Kalispell, Montana. Thanks for living the dream with me! Special thanks to those who helped with this book: Amy Lathrop, Tanya Flores, Jamie Lyn Spaulding, Marjie Shanks, and Nikki Hammond. And to Jeannie for cooking for me! And thanks to Lynsie for helping me with the title!

Thanks to my writing friends who prayed me through this project: OH Ladies, BH Friends, and AWSA Girls. And to fellow writers who read every word and urged me to a higher standard: Ocieanna Fleiss, Marlo Schalesky, and Mike Yorkey. You're great!

Hats off to Beth Lagerborg from MOPS; my editors at Zondervan, Sandy Vander Zicht and Brian Phipps; and my agent, Janet Kobobel Grant. I appreciate your making it possible to reach teen moms with this message!

I especially appreciate the help from teen moms around the *world* who offered their unique insights. Especially those I quote in this book: Amanda, Desiree, Diana, Jessica H., Jessica K., Jessica R., Katherine, Laticia, Leanne, Nancy, Nina, Sarah, Simone, Travis, and Tricia.

Hats off to the MOPS organization and the wonderful ministry you offer to *all* mothers. I especially want to acknowledge Elisa Morgan and Carol Kuykendall. I am indebted to the research and expertise you put into discovering a mom's nine basic needs and producing the wonderful resource *What Every Mom Needs*. When I began this project, my tentative title was *What Every Teen Mom Needs*. The vision and the inspiration to create a book specifically for young moms would not have been possible without the strong foundation you allowed me to build on. Thank you!

Finally, all the glory goes to my Savior, Jesus, for seeking me out and transforming my life. Where would I be without you?

notes

chapter 1: do I matter? (importance)

1. Author unknown, quoted in *Chicken Soup for the Mother's Soul* (Dearfield Beach, Fla.: Health Communications, 2001), 95.
2. Jacqueline Kennedy Onassis, "Women's Voices: Quotations by Women" (http://womenshistory.about.com/library/qu/blquonas.htm).
3. Elisa Morgan, *God's Words of Life for Moms* (Grand Rapids, Mich., Inspiro, 2000), 43. Used with permission.
4. *Early Brain Development in Children and Learning,* http://www.aap.org/mrt/brain.htm.
5. Tricia McKinley. Used with permission.
6. William Sears, Martha Sears, Joyce Warman, et al. From *Parent Project: Tools for Godly Parenting* quoted in *Lists to Live By for Every Caring Family* (Sisters, Ore.: Multnomah, 2001), 107. Used with permission.

chapter 2: who am I? (identity)

1. *WordNet ® 1.6, © 1997 Princeton University.*
2. Jay McGraw, *Life Strategies for Teens Workbook* (New York: Simon and Schuster, 2001), 52.
3. Andrea J. Buchanan, *Mother Shock: Tales from the First Year and Beyond* (New York: Seal Press, 2003), 62.
4. Elisa Morgan and Carol Kuykendall, *What Every Mom Needs* (Grand Rapids, Mich.: Zondervan, 1995), 44.
5. Psalm 139:13.
6. Zephaniah 3:17.
7. Song of Songs 4:9.
8. John 3:16.
9. Michael Hodgin, *1001 Humorous Illustrations for Public Speaking* (Grand Rapids, Mich.: Zondervan, 1994), 595. Used with permission.
10. "100 Leading National Advertisers," *Advertising Age,* (September 28, 1999), S1–S46.

chapter 3: where am I going? (growth)

1. Peter DeVries, as quoted in *TakeCare* (The Hope Heart Institute newsletter), June 2003.
2. Michael Hodgin, *1001 More Humorous Illustrations for Public Speaking* (Grand Rapids, Mich.: Zondervan, 1998), 98. Used with permission.
3. MOPS International, *Mom Email*, 18 November 2003.
4. Hodgin, *1001 More Humorous Illustrations*, 44. Used with permission.
5. Barbara Sher, *Wishcraft: How to Get What You Really Want* (New York: Viking Press, 1979), 15.
6. Wilber and Orville Wright, http://www.wam.umd.edu/~stwright/WrBr/Wrights.html.
7. Dannah Gresh, *Secret Keeper: The Delicate Power of Modesty* (Chicago: Moody Publishing, 2002), 23.
8. Ephesians 1:11 (MESSAGE).
9. Check out free on-line training for your GED (General Educational Development) certificate at http://litlink.ket.org/learn.iphtml or http://www.4tests.com/.
10. Les Parrott and Neil Clark Warren, *Love the Life You Live* (Carol Stream, Ill.: Tyndale, 2003), 29.
11. Frank Outlaw, quoted in *Lists to Live By for Everything That Really Matters*, compiled by Alice Gray, Steve Stephens, and John van Diest (Sisters, Ore., Multnomah, 1999), 69.
12. Mike Pierron, www.drmbig.com/. Used with permission.

chapter 4: do you love me? (intimacy)

1. *Adolescence Magazine,* on-line: http://www.findarticles.com/cf_0/m2248/139_35/68535842/p2/article.jhtml?term=%2BTeenage+%2Bmothers+%2BPsychology+%2Band+%2Bmental+%2Bhealth.
2. Elisa Morgan, *God's Word of Life for Moms* (Grand Rapids: Mich.: Zondervan, 2000), 85. Used with permission.
3. Andrea J. Buchanan, *Mother Shock: Tales from the First Year and Beyond* (New York: Seal Press, 2003), 1.
4. Dorothy Madden, as quoted in *TakeCare* (The Hope Heart Institute newsletter), June 2003.
5. James M. Barrie, quoted in *Patches of Godlight* by Jan Karon (New York, Penguin Putnam, 2001), 56.
6. Morgan, *God's Words of Life,* 85. Used with permission.
7. Ruth Bell Graham, quoted in *Stories for the Family's Heart,* compiled by Alice Gray (Sisters, Ore.: Multnomah, 1998), 128.
8. *Cosmogirl,* May 2003.
9. Heritage Foundation, based on data from the National Longitudinal Survey of Adolescent Health, a nationwide survey that examined behaviors of

adolescents in junior high and high school. (Family Research Council, Press Release, 3 June 2003.) www.frc.org.

10. *Washington Update* press release ("New Study Redefines the Age of Innocence," Wednesday, 21 May 2003).

11. Michael Hodgin, *1001 Humorous Illustrations for Public Speaking* (Grand Rapids, Mich.: Zondervan, 1994), 229. Used with permission.

12. Jo-Ellen Dimitrius, *Reading People* (New York: Random House, 1998), 13.

13. Author unknown, Shine website, http://www.neloo.com/shine/quotes1.html.

14. Elisa Morgan and Carol Kuykendall, *What Every Mom Needs* (Grand Rapids, Mich.: Zondervan, 1995), 87.

15. Carole Mayhall, condensed from "Lord, Teach Me Wisdom" quoted in *Lists to Live By for Everything That Really Matters,* compiled by Alice Gray, Steve Stephens, and John van Diest (Sisters, Ore.: Multnomah, 1999), 123. Used with permission.

16. Al Gray and Alice Gray, in *Lists to Live By,* 119. Used with permission.

chapter 5: how do I do this mom thing? (instruction)

1. Andrea J. Buchanan, *Mother Shock: Tales from the First Year and Beyond* (New York: Seal Press, 2003), 54.

2. Ibid., x.

3. Ibid., 7.

4. Quoted in Heather Hurd, *A Book of Hope for Mothers* (Nashville: The Wisdom Company, 2000), 7.

5. Charles R. Swindoll, *Growing Strong in the Seasons of Life* (Grand Rapids, Mich.: Zondervan, 1983), 290. Used with permission.

6. Antonio Porchia, quoted in Hurd, *A Book of Hope for Mothers,* 21.

7. Patti MacGregor, from "Family Times: Growing Together in Fun and Faith," quoted in *Lists to Live By for Everything That Really Matters* (Sisters, Ore.: Multnomah, 1999), 313. Used with permission.

8. Proverbs 15:17.

9. Proverbs 15:18.

10. Proverbs 15:22.

11. Proverbs 16:3.

12. Proverbs 17:17.

13. Proverbs 18:13.

14. Proverbs 3:5.

15. Proverbs 3:6.

16. Robert Bender, *Never Eat Anything That Moves: Good, Bad, and Very Silly Advice from Kids* (New York: Dial Books for Young Readers, 2002).

17. Author unknown, quoted in *Lists to Live By for Everything That Really Matters* (Sisters, Ore.: Multnomah, 1999), 315.

chapter 6: can you help? (help)

1. Michael Hodgin, *1001 More Humorous Illustrations for Public Speaking* (Grand Rapids, Mich.: Zondervan, 1998), 42. Used with permission.
2. Julie Ann Barnhill, *She's Gonna Blow! Real Help for Moms Dealing with Anger* (Eugene, Ore.: Harvest House, 2001), 176.
3. Elisa Morgan, *God's Words of Life for Moms* (Grand Rapids, Mich.: Inspiro, 2000), 17. Used with permission.
4. Sarah, Sydney, Australia.
5. Michael Hodgin, *1001 Humorous Illustrations for Public Speaking* (Grand Rapids, Mich.: Zondervan, 1994), 316. Used with permission. Used with permission.
6. Andrea Engber and Leah Klungness, *The Complete Single Mother* (Holbrook, Mass.: Adams Publishing, 1995), 41.
7. Ibid., 99. Copyright © 1995, 2000 Andrea Engber and Leah Klungness. Used with permission of Adams Media. All rights reserved.
8. Helen Keller, quoted in *Patches of Godlight* by Jan Karon (New York: Penguin Putnam, 2001), 11.
9. Sarah, Sydney, Australia.
10. WIC is the Special Supplemental Nutritional Program for Women, Infants, and Children; see www.fns.usda.gov/wic/. For more information on Teen MOPS, see "The MOPS Story" at the end of this book.
11. Hodgin, *1001 More Humorous Illustrations,* 661. Used with permission.
12. Dan Clark, quoted in *Chicken Soup for the Mother's Soul: 101 Stories to Open the Hearts and Rekindle the Spirits of Mothers* (Deerfield Beach, Fla.: Health Communications, 1997), 203. Used with permission.
13. Brenda Nixon, www.parentpwr.com.

chapter 7: I need a break (recreation)

1. Michael Hodgin, *1001 Humorous Illustrations for Public Speaking* (Grand Rapids, Mich.: Zondervan, 1994), 316. Used with permission.
2. 1997 by Elaine Hardt. Hardt Ministries International, Inc. 4700 Scout Way, Prescott Valley, AZ 86314. Used with permission.
3. Sylvia Harney, *Everytime I Go Home, I Break Out in Relatives* (Nashville: Word, 1990), 123.
4. *Simple Truths for Moms* (Lincolnwood, Ill.: New Seasons Publishers, 2001), 5.
5. Heather Hurd, Kathy Knight, and Cecil O. Kemp Jr., eds., *A Book of Hope for Mothers* (Nashville: Wisdom Company, 2000).
6. Amanda, Ontario, Canada.
7. Julie Ann Barnhill, *She's Gonna Blow! Real Help for Moms Dealing with Anger* (Eugene, Ore.: Harvest House, 2001), 176.
8. Simone, New Zealand.
9. Diana, Washington.

10. Travis, Michigan.
11. Travis, Michigan.
12. Diane and Rob Parsons, *The Sixty Minute Mother* (Nashville: Broadman and Holman, 2002), 102. Used with permission.
13. Hodgin, *1001 Humorous Illustrations,* 606. Used with permission.
14. Michael Hodgin, *1001 More Humorous Illustrations for Public Speaking* (Grand Rapids, Mich.: Zondervan, 1998), 707. Used with permission.
15. Ibid., 734. Used with permission.
16. Karyn Henley, from *HomeLife Magazine,* quoted in *Lists to Live By for Every Caring Family* (Sisters, Ore.: Multnomah, 2001), 68–69. Used with permission.

chapter 8: what's most important? (perspective)

1. Michael Hodgin, *1001 Humorous Illustrations for Public Speaking* (Grand Rapids, Mich.: Zondervan, 1994), 642. Used with permission.
2. Lucinda Bassett, *Life without Limits* (New York: Cliff Street Books, 2001), 187.
3. Sean Covey, *The Seven Habits of Highly Effective Teens* (New York: Fireside Books, 1998). Used with permission.
4. Author unknown, quoted in *Lists to Live By for Everything That Really Matters,* compiled by Alice Gray, Steve Stephens, and John van Diest (Sisters, Ore.: Multnomah, 1999), 317.
5. Joanna Weaver, *Having a Mary Heart in a Martha World* (Colorado Springs, Colo.: WaterBrook, 2002), 184.
6. Sark, *Succulent, Wild Woman: Dancing with Your Wonderful Self* (New York: Simon Schuster, 1997), 117.
7. Author unknown, *Stories for the Family's Heart,* compiled by Alice Gray (Sisters, Ore.: Multnomah, 1998), 179.

chapter 9: what am I here for? (hope)

1. Emily Dickinson, *Selected Poems and Letters of Emily Dickenson,* Robert N. Linscott, ed. (Garden City: Doubleday Anchor, 1959), 79.
2. Laticia, Oklahoma.
3. Ken Gire, *The Divine Embrace: An Invitation to the Dance of Intimacy with Christ One Exhilarating, Ennobling, Uncertain Step at a Time* (Carol Stream, Ill.: Tyndale, 2003). Used with permission.
4. John Van Diest, *Lists to Live By for Everything That Really Matters,* compiled by Alice Gray, Steve Stephens, and John van Diest (Sisters, Ore.: Multnomah, 1999), 206. Used with permission.
5. Michael Hodgin, *1001 More Humorous Illustrations for Public Speaking* (Grand Rapids, Mich.: Zondervan, 1998), 720. Used with permission.

for further reading

chapter 1: do I matter? (importance)

Morgan, Elisa and Carol Kuykendall. *What Every Child Needs*. Grand Rapids, Mich.: Zondervan, 2000.

> Your child needs things such as love and security to build a good foundation in life. You are important for meeting those needs. This book will provide you with sound advice and encouragement.

Morgan, Elisa, ed., Laurie Snow Hein, illus. *A Love Like No Other*. Sisters, Ore.: Multnomah, 2001.

> A mother's love for her child may well be the strongest bond on earth. In their own words, mothers throughout the country share their concerns and joys, their victories and trials, and their treasured memories of mothering. This collection of personal tales will encourage you.

chapter 2: who am I? (identity)

McGraw, Jay. *Life Strategies for Teens Workbook*. New York: Simon and Schuster, 2001.

> A fun-filled book that introduces a variety of entertaining quizzes, activities, and questions to help you discover who you are. From figuring out the roles you play, to determining the things you want to change about your life, this guide will show you how to take control of your life.

Littauer, Florence. *Personality Plus: How to Understand Others by Understanding Yourself*. Grand Rapids, Mich.: Revell, 1992.

> This interesting book provides keys to understanding yourself and those around you. You'll learn how to accept—and even enjoy—the traits that make each of us different.

Kise, Jane A. G. and Kevin Walter Johnson. *Find Your Fit: Dare to Act on Who You Are.* Minneapolis: Bethany House, 1999.

> What do you want to be when you grow up? This is a great tool to help you discover your talents, values, passions, and personality type.

chapter 3: where am I going? (growth)

Trent, John T. *Making Wise Life Choices.* Carol Stream, Ill.: Tyndale, 2003.

> This book has practical tips to help you make wise decisions and create healthy habits that will better your life and your relationships.

Covey, Sean. *The Seven Habits of Highly Effective Teens.* New York: Simon and Schuster, 1998.

> A step-by-step guide to help you improve your self-image, build friendships, resist peer pressure, achieve your goals, get along with your parents, and much more. In addition, this book is stuffed with cartoons, clever ideas, great quotes, and incredible stories about real teens from all over the world.

Parsons, Rob and Dianne Parsons. *The 60 Minute Mother.* Nashville: Broadman and Holman, 2002.

> Encouragement from other moms as they share *their* joys, fears, laughter, and frustrations! Chapters include "The Greatest Gift You Can Give Your Child," "I Think I'm a Good Mom, So Why Do I Sometimes Feel So Guilty?" and "Single Moms: The Challenge and the Hope."

chapter 4: do you love me? (intimacy)

Tirabassi, Becky and Roger Tirabassi. *How to Live with Them: Since You Can't Live without Them.* Nashville: Thomas Nelson, 1998.

> You marry the person you just can't live without. Then you discover that living with that person can be pretty tough too. This book includes interactive questions, how-to's, guidelines, and even homework assignments that will help you live with and love your partner.

Arterburn, Stephen and Dr. Meg J. Rinck. *Avoiding Mr. Wrong (And What to Do If You Didn't).* Nashville: Thomas Nelson, 2001.

> Maybe you're dating him . . . the Detached Man. Or the Deceiver. Or the Control Freak — or countless, unhealthy variations of him. If so, here's practical help for breaking those negative patterns once and for all. This insightful book

will help you spot the bad guys and learn why you're drawn to them. Even if you think you've already married Mr. Wrong, it's not too late.

Understanding yourself and your spouse better is the first step to helping your Mr. Wrong become Mr. Right.

Lookadoo, Justin and Hayley Morgan. *Dateable: Are You? Are They?* Grand Rapids, Mich.: Revell, 2003.

Clueless about the opposite sex? This book exposes the inside world of guys and girls. It also gives helpful advice on having an internal sense of confidence, control, and sexuality that will help you discover your "date-ability."

chapter 5: how do I do this mom thing? (instruction)

Nixon, Brenda. *Parenting Power in the Early Years: Raising Your Child with Confidence—Birth to Age Five.* Enumclaw, Wash.: WinePress, 2001.

A great resource for moms who are raising young kids. This book covers how to be a successful parent with topics such as, "When to start solid foods," "When to begin toilet teaching," "How to handle tantrums or biting," and more!

Barnhill, Julie Ann. *She's Gonna Blow! Real Help for Moms Dealing with Anger.* Eugene, Ore.: Harvest House, 2001.

A "been there, done that" mom uses everyday life with young children to illustrate the painful realities of what happens when anger is mismanaged. This book will give you honest understanding, wise biblical counsel, and hope for lasting change.

Arp, David and Claudia Arp. *New Baby Stress.* Carol Stream, Ill.: Tyndale, 2003.

This book will give you ideas for how to get enough rest, develop a parenting style that's uniquely suited to you, communicate effectively about the things that really matter, and even rekindle your love life with your spouse.

chapter 6: can you help? (help)

Vernick, Leslie. *How to Act Right When Your Spouse Acts Wrong.* Colorado Springs, Colo.: WaterBrook, 2003.

This book is important for every married person. It will give you advice for what to do whenever your spouse disappoints you, fails you, hurts you, or just plain irritates you.

Sumner, Cynthia. *Mommy's Locked in the Bathroom: Surviving Your Child's Early Years with Your Sanity and Salvation Intact!* Uhrichsville, Ohio: Barbour, 2003.

> A humorous and practical guide to surviving the stresses of motherhood. This book will give you ideas for small things that will make a big difference in your energy level.

Freeman, Becky. *Survival Tips for Parents of Preschoolers.* Carol Stream, Ill.: Tyndale, 2003.

> You'll find helpful tips and creative ideas on topics such as finding the rest you need, keeping the house livable on a busy schedule, understanding how your preschooler thinks, and teaching your child about God.

chapter 7: I need a break (recreation)

Shelton, Deborah, Frankie Gordon, illus. *The Five-Minute Parent: Fun and Fast Activities for You and Your Little Ones.* Houston: Bayou, 2001.

> Don't wait for the weekend! Create small treasures and lasting memories with children in just minutes! This book turns five minutes together into a treasury of new experiences neither of you will ever forget.

Radic, Shelly. *The Birthday Book: Creative Ways to Celebrate Your Child's Special Day.* Grand Rapids, Mich.: Zondervan, 2002.

> This book provides a variety of meaningful ways to celebrate birthdays. It includes ideas for invitations, food, games, and activities for birthday parties, and gives age-specific tips, ideas, and complete party plans for children ages one through the elementary school years.

Lagerborg, Mary Beth, ed. *In the Wee Hours: Up-in-the-Nighttime Stories for Mom.* Grand Rapids, Mich.: Zondervan, 2001.

> When you need a little time to relax, this book of short stories, poems, letters, journal entries, anecdotes, and lullabies entertains a mom and gives her perspective with which to end one day and look forward to the next. Each narrative presents a woman dealing with a challenging, sometimes funny, situation.

chapter 8: what's most important? (perspective)

O'Connor, Lindsey. *If Mama Ain't Happy . . . Ain't Nobody Happy: Making the Choice to Rejoice*. Eugene, Ore.: Harvest House, 2003.

Our influence is incredible. As mothers, we are the thermostats in the home, regulating the temperature and atmosphere by our very presence. This book will give you better perspective on how your attitude affects your home.

Morgan, Elisa and Carol Kuykendall. *Real Moms*. Grand Rapids, Mich.: Zondervan, 2002.

Are you tired of constantly trying—and failing—to be a perfect mom? Stop beating yourself up and let the truth about motherhood set you free!

Ladd, Karol. *The Power of a Positive Mom*. West Monroe, La.: Howard, 2001.

You may not look in the mirror everyday and see yourself as having a great influence on the world, but you do! This book will help ensure that your impact is positive.

chapter 9: what am I here for? (hope)

Revolve: The Complete New Testament. Nashville: Thomas Nelson, 2003.

A Bible that looks more like a fashion magazine! With articles on topics that interest you.

Kubiak, Shannon. *The Divine Dance: If the World Is Your Stage . . . Who Are You Performing For?* Uhrichsville, Ohio: Barbour, 2003.

This book confronts issues of image, integrity, dating, family relationships, friendships, and maintaining a personal relationship with Christ in an upfront fashion.

Shellenberger, Susie. *Girl Talk with God*. Nashville: W Publishing, 2001.

This book will show you how to pray and will challenge you to deepen specific areas in your life through a series of conversations between God and a teenage girl.

credits

The poem in chapter 1 titled "Yes, I Am Young" by Tricia McKinley is used with permission.

The material in chapter 1 titled "Messages for Baby" is taken from William Sears, Martha Sears, Joyce Warmna, et al., *Parent Project: Tools for Godly Parenting* (Nashville: LifeWay, 2000). Used with permission.

The material in chapters 1, 4, and 6 quoting *God's Words of Life for Moms* is taken from *God's Words of Life for Moms* by Elisa Morgan. Copyright 2000 by the Zondervan Corporation. Used by permission of the Zondervan Corporation.

The material in chapters 2–4 and 6–8 quoting *1001 Humorous Illustrations for Public Speaking* is taken from *1001 Humorous Illustrations for Public Speaking* by Michael Hodgin. Copyright 1994 by Michael Hodgin. Used by permission of the Zondervan Corporation.

The material in chapter 3 titled "The ABCs of Achieving Your Dreams" by Michael Pierron is used with permission.

The material in chapter 4 titled "Springboards to Deeper Conversation" is condensed from Carole Mayhall, *Lord, Teach Me Wisdom* (Colorado Springs, Colo.: NavPress, 1979). Used with permission.

The material in chapter 4 titled "Eighteen Attributes to Look for in a Marriage Partner" is from Al Gray and Alice Gray, quoted in *Lists to Live By for Everything That Really Matters,* compiled by Alice Gray, Steve Stephens, and John van Diest (Sisters, Ore.: Multnomah, 1999). Used with permission.

The material in chapter 5 quoting *Growing Strong in the Seasons of Life* is taken from *Growing Strong in the Seasons of Life* by Charles R. Swindoll. Copyright 1983 by Charles R. Swindoll, Inc. Used by permission of the Zondervan Corporation.

The material in chapter 5 titled "Wise Things Your Grandma Told You" is from Patti MacGregor, "Family Times: Growing Together in Fun and

the MOPS story

Y ou take care of your children, Mom. Who takes care of you? MOPS International (Mothers of Preschoolers) provides mothers of young children with the help they need to be the best moms they can be. In Teen MOPS groups, MOPS International offers these benefits specifically for pregnant and parenting teens!

MOPS is dedicated to the message that "mothering matters." We know that moms of young children need encouragement. Chartered groups meet in approximately 3,000 churches and Christian ministries throughout the United States and in 22 other countries. Teen MOPS groups also meet in schools and community centers.

Each MOPS program helps mothers find friendship, provides practice in leadership skills, and promotes spiritual growth. Teen MOPS provides a supportive, nonjudging environment where young moms can meet with others in a similar life situation.

The MOPPETS program offers a loving, learning experience for children while their moms attend MOPS. Other MOPS resources include *MOMSense* magazine and radio broadcast, the MOPS International website, and books and resources available through the MOPShop.

There are 14.3 million mothers of preschoolers in the United States alone, many of whom can't attend a local MOPS group. These moms still need the support MOPS International offers! For a small registration fee, any mother of preschoolers can join the MOPS-to-Mom Connection and receive *MOMSense* magazine six times a year, a weekly Mom-E-Mail message of encouragement, and other valuable benefits.

To find out how MOPS International can help you, visit our website at www.MOPS.org. Phone us at 303-733-5353. Or e-mail Info@MOPS.org. To learn how to start a MOPS or Teen MOPS group, call 1-888-910-MOPS.

What Every Mom Needs

Meet Your Nine Basic Needs (and Be a Better Mom)

Elisa Morgan and Carol Kuykendall

"Do I ever get to be someone besides 'Mom'?" Sound familiar? You're not selfish; you're normal. And like every mother, you have nine basic needs—significance, identity, growth, recreation, and five others identified by MOPS® International after more than twenty years of research and experience.

Now MOPS authors Elisa Morgan and Carol Kuykendall show you how meeting those needs will not only make you more content, it'll make you a better mom. *What Every Mom Needs* is not just another book on parenting. It's a whole-person approach to balanced living that reveals different ways you, the nurturer, also need to be nurtured. Based on sound biblical principles and responses to over 1,000 questionnaires, *What Every Mom Needs* will help you expand your personal horizons and become a better mom in the bargain.

Softcover: 0-310-21920-5

What Every Child Needs

Meet Your Child's Nine Basic Needs for Love

Elisa Morgan and Carol Kuykendall

Drawing on the latest research and on the insights of moms across America, *What Every Child Needs* helps mothers meet their children's nine basic needs for security, affirmation, belonging, discipline, guidance, respect, play, independence, and hope. Using a child's language of love, Elisa Morgan and Carol Kuykendall of MOPS International show how moms can meet each need ... and respect their own needs in the process. Seasoned with poignant stories and wise quotes from moms, this book will encourage mothers that the person they are is the mom their child needs.

Softcover: 0-310-23271-6

Mom's Health Matters

Practical Answers to Your Top Health Concerns

Carrie Carter, M.D.

Carrie Carter, M.D.

Are you so busy taking care of your family that you're forgetting to take care of yourself?

Written by a pediatrician, this easy-to-use handbook gives you practical ways to create a vibrantly healthy lifestyle that gives you abundant daily energy and prevents disease. You'll find answers to questions such as:

- How do I get more energy?
- Which healthy weight-loss strategies really work?
- What nutritional supplements should I be taking?
- How can I keep from feeling stressed and overwhelmed by the demands of family life?
- What methods of birth control are safe for me?
- What can I do about fluctuating hormones and changes in libido?
- When is it normal "baby blues" and when is it a more serious form of depression?
- Who is the right doctor for me? For my children?

This book is full of practical tips for improving and maintaining your health. Just what the doctor ordered for moms on the go, *Mom's Health Matters* will help you stay healthy, live longer, and feel better.

Softcover: 0-310-24743-8

ZONDERVAN™

GRAND RAPIDS, MICHIGAN 49530 USA

WWW.ZONDERVAN.COM

Real Moms
Exploding the Myths of Motherhood

Elisa Morgan and Carol Kuykendall

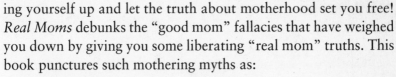

MOM! GET REAL . . . AND GET FREE!

Are you tired of constantly trying—and failing—to be a perfect mom? Stop beating yourself up and let the truth about motherhood set you free! *Real Moms* debunks the "good mom" fallacies that have weighed you down by giving you some liberating "real mom" truths. This book punctures such mothering myths as:

- Good moms look good all the time.
- Good moms keep everybody happy.
- Good moms instinctively know what their children need.
- Good moms take responsibility for how their children turn out.
- Good moms don't admit their feelings of guilt or anger or fear—because to admit those feelings might make them look like they are not good moms.

Each chapter examines a myth and its corresponding reality and ends with a how-to practical application, a "Real Mom" story, questions for reflection and discussion, and "Real Mom" quotes from real mothers.

Wouldn't you love to be free to accept your imperfections? Free not to feel guilty about your limitations? Free to ask for help, free to be real, free to grow? Freedom is in store for you—freedom to be the best mom you can be. This book will show you the way.

Softcover: 0-310-24703-9

We want to hear from you. Please send your comments about this book to us in care of zreview@zondervan.com. Thank you.

GRAND RAPIDS, MICHIGAN 49530 USA

WWW.ZONDERVAN.COM